WAKING THE SLEEPING GIANT

WAKING THE SLEEPING GIANT

HOW MAINSTREAM AMERICANS CAN BEAT LIBERALS AT THEIR OWN GAME

TIMOTHY C. DAUGHTRY, PhD

AND

GARY R. CASSELMAN, PhD

BEAUFORT
BOOKS

Copyright © 2012 by Timothy C. Daughtry, PhD and Gary R. Casselman, PhD

FIRST EDITION

Library of Congress Cataloging-in-Publication Data

Daughtry, Timothy C.

Waking the sleeping giant : how mainstream Americans can beat liberals at their own game / Timothy C. Daughtry and Gary R. Casselman. —1st ed.

　　p. cm.

Includes bibliographical references and index.

ISBN 978-0-8253-0679-2 (alk. paper)

1. Conservatism—United States. 2. Liberalism—United States. 3. United States—Politics and government—2009- I. Casselman, Gary R. II. Title.

JC573.2.U6D38 2012

320.520973—dc23

　　　　　　2011043229

For inquiries about volume orders, please contact:

Beaufort Books
27 West 20th Street, Suite 1102
New York, NY 10011
sales@beaufortbooks.com

Published in the United States by Beaufort Books
www.beaufortbooks.com

Distributed by Midpoint Trade Books
www.midpointtrade.com

Printed in the United States of America
Interior design by Maria E. Torres, Neuwirth & Associates, Inc.
Cover Design by Tobias Design

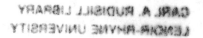

DEDICATION

TO OUR CHILDREN

EVER SINCE the founding of the greatest nation in history, each successive generation of Americans have enjoyed an increasingly better quality of life in every dimension—economic, social, and personal. This occurred because of the decisions made by the preceding generation operating within the parameters of a capitalist economic system and a free and open society, based on the principles laid forth by our Founding Fathers in the Constitution.

As discussed in this book, because of the slow erosion of our liberty over approximately the last hundred years with the long march through the institutions, we are at the precipice of a change that will last forever. For the first time in our history, this generation of baby boomers could very well leave a nation to our children that is less free, less prosperous, and with less opportunity than we enjoyed and, quite frankly, took for granted.

With the horrific policies coming out of Washington, D.C., in the past three years, we have seen an exponential increase in our loss of liberty, in the loss of American exceptionalism, in the loss of the value of the American dollar, in the size of government, in unemployment, and in the size of the welfare state, with its concomitant sense of entitlement.

Part of our purpose in writing this book was to do what we could to create the conditions required, along with millions of other patriotic Americans, to reverse the trends of the past fifty to one hundred years. If we are to avoid being the first generation of Americans who pass on to their children a country that offers less—less freedom, less opportunity, less prosperity—we must stop the progressive, leftist movement.

It is to our children, all of our children, and our children's children, that we dedicate this book. With guidance from God and with the help of our fellow mainstream Americans, we can return our country to the constitutional republic that was the dream of our Founding Fathers and has been the envy of the world for a hundred years.

If we fail, with the passing of the baby boom generation, perhaps the last generation to enjoy the American dream of our forefathers, this country will reach a tipping point, and the America we love and cherish will be lost forever.

CONTENTS

ACKNOWLEDGMENTS

THE AUTHORS gratefully acknowledge the wisdom and guidance of Eric Kampmann and Margot Atwell of Beaufort Books in the production and distribution of this book. Without their help, the book would have remained in draft form for years to come. We also want to thank Sarah Lucie and Oriana Leckert for their painstaking editing in bringing the manuscript to completion.

Ernie and Joanne Wittenborn also deserve special thanks for their tireless work in the grassroots movement to restore the republic and for opening the doors that made publication of this book possible.

Finally, Dr. Daughtry would like to thank Judy and Jacob for their encouragement and patience during this project and for serving as constant inspiration to stay in the struggle to save our country.

1

WAKING THE SLEEPING GIANT

"I fear all we have done is to awaken a sleeping giant and fill him with a terrible resolve."

—Attributed to Admiral Isoroku Yamamoto after the
Japanese attack on Pearl Harbor

THE END OF THE AMERICAN REPUBLIC?

The American republic is teetering on the edge of a precipice. America has faced and survived crises before, but the economic and political crisis that came to a head in 2010 and 2011 is unprecedented in its scope and implications.

We cannot count on politicians to put America back on a sound course. Unless mainstream citizens, the sleeping giant of American politics, wake up and take the helm of this country soon, the current generation will be the last to live in freedom.

If an American collapse seems unthinkable, just remember that the world witnessed something just as unthinkable in 1991 with the breakup of the Soviet Union. For those of us who grew up with the constant threat of a nuclear war with this dark and mysterious entity, the Soviet Union seemed permanent—a sinister, monolithic, totalitarian state that contended with the United States in every arena around the globe. And then, within a matter of weeks, the Soviet Union and its centrally controlled economy lay on the ash heap of history.

When the economic and political rot of communism finally caused the evil empire to crumble from within, it was a reminder of something most of us learned from the cradle: Our ideas and our actions have consequences.[1] Centralized control of economic activity, whether by communists in Moscow or leftists in Washington, is as arrogant as it is unworkable. The old Soviet joke that "we pretend to work and they pretend to pay us" sums up the predictable consequences of economic and political actions that are out of touch with the reality of human nature.

The collapse of the Soviet Union proved once more the wisdom in Rudyard Kipling's poem "The Gods of the Copybook Headings":

> *In the Carboniferous Epoch, we were promised abundance for all,*
> *By robbing selected Peter to pay for collective Paul;*
> *But, though we had plenty of money, there was nothing our money could buy,*
> *And the Gods of the Copybook Headings said: "If you don't work you die."*[2]

AMERICA'S ECONOMIC CRISIS

With almost half of the electorate paying no income taxes to fund the government that they empower with their votes, the United States is on the verge of learning, as did the Soviet Union, the consequences of "robbing selected Peter to pay for collective Paul."[3] In fact, the damage wrought by leftist policies in much of Europe could have served as a lesson and a warning to America's political class, if they had been willing to learn.

We can ignore the lessons of nature and of history, but we cannot avoid the consequences of doing so. As Benjamin Franklin warned us, "Experience holds a dear school, but a fool will learn in no other."

In 2011, when Standard & Poor's downgraded America's credit rating for the first time in our history, it became undeniable that this economic crisis was like no other. The government spending money it did not have—and promising abundance for all—had long been a way of life inside the Beltway. But for the first time, the world questioned not just the ability of our government to pay its tab but also whether our government had the political wisdom and maturity to do so.

AMERICA'S POLITICAL CRISIS

The lessons of leftist policies in the Soviet Union, Greece, Ireland, Italy, Portugal, and Spain were there for anyone to see, yet our government kept spending as if the tab would never come due. Mainstream citizens knew what was wrong, but other than voting, we did not know how to fix it. Mainstream Americans work, take care of our responsibilities, pay our taxes, and vote. After we vote, we go back home and trust our elected officials to work within their constitutional boundaries.

But trusting elected officials to voluntarily limit their appetite for power is like trusting a dog to guard your dinner. The political incentives of elective office promote neither fiscal responsibility nor limited government. Like lords of a feudal manor, politicians dispense largesse from the public treasury to their voters and interest groups, and those voters and interest groups return the favor by keeping those politicians in positions of wealth and power. That, in a nutshell, is the political crisis that took America from the healthiest economy on earth to being trillions of dollars in debt.

As an example, remember the arrogance of Nancy Pelosi's statement about Obamacare: "We have to pass the bill so that you can see what is in it." Harry Reid pushed the bill through the Senate with minimal debate, and Barack Obama celebrated his first major victory. But then, as mainstream Americans who had opposed Obamacare struggled to comprehend the damage it would cause to their businesses and their personal health plans, the largest constituents and contributors to leftist causes got Obamacare waivers.[4]

Benjamin Franklin is often credited with the statement, "When the people find they can vote themselves money, that will herald the end of the republic." That is, the system works just fine for those distributing the money and for those receiving it until, as Margaret Thatcher warned, "Eventually, you run out of other people's money."

But our current crisis goes beyond having a central government that is essentially bankrupt and still growing. The grasp of governmental power reaches into more and more aspects of our lives. Reckless spending is merely one result of that grasp.

Yet, dire though it may be, there is nothing especially surprising about America's economic and political crisis. Our Founding Fathers described what would happen if the citizens did not remain vigilant, if we refused to benefit from the wisdom of the ages. And now that our politicians have run out of other people's money, the gods of Kipling's copybook headings loom large on our political horizon, reminding us that no amount of silver-tongued talk about "hope" and "change" can alter the way the world really works:

Then the Gods of the Market tumbled, and their smooth-tongued wizards withdrew
And the hearts of the meanest were humbled and began to believe it was true
That All is not Gold that Glitters, and Two and Two make Four
And the Gods of the Copybook Headings limped up to explain it once more.

As it will be in the future, it was at the birth of Man—
There are only four things certain since Social Progress began—
That the Dog returns to his Vomit and the Sow returns to her Mire,
And the burnt Fool's bandaged finger goes wobbling back to the Fire;

And that after this is accomplished, and the brave new world begins
When all men are paid for existing and no man must pay for his sins,
As surely as Water will wet us, as surely as Fire will burn,
The Gods of the Copybook Headings with terror and slaughter return!

We have seen riots in the streets of Europe as leftist governments ran out of other people's money and the false promise of easy abundance was broken, as it inevitably will be. There is a price for ignoring the lessons of history, and that price is slow decline at best, and chaos and collapse at worst.

THE ROOTS OF THE CRISIS: CULTURE AND CHARACTER

The survival of the United States is no more assured than that of the former Soviet Union. But the economic and political crises we face now are only symptoms of a deeper problem.

We were once the greatest nation on earth, not because there was anything especially deserving about the people of this country but because our political and economic system was exceptional. The Founding Fathers who created our system demonstrated profound understanding of human nature, the lessons of history, and the wisdom handed down in our Judeo-Christian worldview.

Our system worked because of the worldview on which it was based. That worldview shaped the culture of our country and the character of our people, and the crisis of our republic is a result of a deeper crisis in our cultural institutions and in the character of our people.

THE CULTURAL FOUNDATIONS OF LIBERTY

It is worth noting here that the title of Kipling's poem is drawn from the old copybook method of teaching children to read and write. Children once copied wise aphorisms into their copybooks, and as a result they absorbed the wisdom of previous generations as they mastered the mechanics of writing. In *Straight Shooting: What's Wrong with America and How to Fix It,* John Silber reviewed those aphorisms and the deeper life lessons they conveyed as part of the normal process of educating children.[5]

Compare that method of teaching with a popular view today, which holds that as long as children learn the mechanics of reading, the actual reading material does not matter. A comic book is as good as the classics. It took centuries to develop the wisdom that was once transmitted to the next generation by methods such as the copybook. It took one generation to replace that wisdom with comic books. The point here is not about how we teach children to read and write in the age of computers. Technology changes, but wisdom does not, and we are failing to pass on the worldview and the wisdom on which our liberty rests.

In many ways, the political struggle in America is actually a battle between two competing worldviews, one of which leads to liberty, the other of which leads to statism. The problem is that, with very few exceptions, only one side understands that there is a battle going on.

In the early 1900s, leftist intellectuals realized that the way to political power was not through the violent revolution predicted by classical Marxists but through a gradual revolution within the cultural institutions on which political power rests. By undermining the Judeo-Christian foundations of Western civilization and replacing their teachings with a leftist worldview in our schools, newsrooms, and entertainment institutions, those cultural institutions would become the instruments of gradual revolution.

The Judeo-Christian worldview has as its ultimate authority a Creator who has endowed us with certain inalienable rights. Because we are created beings, we have inherent importance. We are also moral beings, and are thus morally accountable for our actions. We are taught to work for what we get. Charity is a moral obligation, and therefore it has to be voluntary. In this worldview, some things are true and some are false. Some truths are considered timeless.

In the Judeo-Christian worldview, human beings are morally imperfect, and any political system created by human hands will reflect this imperfection. In this worldview, everything we call social progress is in reality technical progress. The twelve Americans who landed on the moon had the latest technology available to them, but their moral natures were no different than those of the people Moses led out of Egypt. In the Judeo-Christian worldview, human nature is not perfectible through our own actions. Our ultimate hope comes from the submission of our wills to that of our Creator.

Our constitutional republic, with its respect for individual liberty and its limitations on governmental power, rests on the foundation of this Judeo-Christian worldview.

In the leftist worldview, human life is a result of random chemical processes. We are accidental beings, not created ones. Our worth, and even the meaning of our existence, are arbitrary. All standards of morality are socially constructed; there is no ultimate standard by which to decide issues of right and wrong. Political rights are arbitrary behavioral norms developed to serve the interests of those in power. As such, those rights can be changed by the people in charge. New rights can be invented and old rights discarded to suit the preferences and the convenience of those in power.

The leftist worldview, with its moral relativism, shapes the character of its adherents. When people cut ties to any truth that transcends their own opinions and desires, they are free to drift wherever their impulses and whims take them. And with a robust free-enterprise economy and democratic elections, those impulses and whims will draw them inexorably toward the public treasury. Leftist politicians can count on a core of voters whose sense of entitlement makes them easy prey for politicians who promise easy abundance.

The left's strategy has proven to be a stunning success, if declining educational performance and a $15 trillion debt can be considered success. Leftist thinking dominates our cultural institutions, and those institutions decide what will be discussed in public and how. Control of national discussion—"the narrative," in popular parlance—is why Joseph Biden could compare Tea Party representatives elected in 2010 to terrorists without igniting a storm of challenges from the news media.[6] Had the values of mainstream America prevailed in the newsrooms, any politician making a statement that unspeakably arrogant about representatives just elected in a landslide would have been hounded from office.

The strategy and tactics that we present in this book work from the assumption that our economic and political crises are merely symptoms of that deeper crisis, the weakening of our culture and our national character. We also work from a second assumption that much of America still holds to the essentials of the Judeo-Christian worldview, with its emphasis on the worth and dignity of individuals, personal responsibility, and a healthy skepticism about politicians who promise glittering new solutions to the age-old challenges of life.

Leftist rhetoric is sweet, but the underlying worldview is a different matter altogether. One of the major tactics in this book will be to recognize and expose that underlying worldview so that the left's false promises lose their appeal.

If the American republic is to be restored, if America is to become great again, it will not occur because professional politicians woke up to reality. It will be because the sleeping giant of the American mainstream woke up and remembered a forgotten truth: We are the guardians of the constitutional republic, and the power to restore it lies within us.

That power lies not just in our sheer numbers but also in the power of our ideas. The challenge for mainstream America will be to get our ideas heard in the midst of the leftist din coming from the cultural institutions.

But we will face an even greater challenge: Mainstream Americans are not by nature political animals, and we desperately need to change that.

THE SLEEPING GIANT

Despite our overwhelming numbers, mainstream America has for too long been the sleeping giant of American politics. As mainstream

Americans, we mind our own business, take care of our own responsibilities, play by the rules, and respect the rights of others to live their lives as they choose, as long as they don't harm others.

Those are the character traits of emotionally mature, civilized adults. Mainstream Americans know that families cannot borrow and spend their way to economic health, and we know that the same principle applies to government. We know there is no quick and easy path to personal success or to national prosperity. We know that forcing taxpayers to bail out badly run business is unfair to businesses that are run well, and it is inefficient as well. We know that there is no easy path to responsible home ownership, that the bills must ultimately be paid one way or another, and that our actions, not our intentions, produce results.

In short, all the lessons of "The Gods of the Copybook Headings" are familiar to us.

Winning the Debate While Losing the Republic

Conservatives have won the battle of ideas. Conservative writers like Sean Hannity, Walter Williams, Ann Coulter, Thomas Sowell, Mark Levin, Glenn Beck, and others routinely document the failure of liberal policies and the superiority of conservative ideas, but it is difficult to name a single bestseller arguing that government knows best. Rush dominates the air while Air America died for lack of interest.

Conservatives own the intellectual turf of politics. Some conservative bestsellers have documented what liberalism has done to liberty, to the economy, to our social foundations, and to our prestige and influence abroad. Others have offered ideas about what mainstream America must do to restore legitimate constitutional government.

We know what's wrong with our country, and we know that leftist policies are the problem. But what none have addressed so far is why the mainstream majority has been losing our country even as we have won the battle of ideas.

The Mainstream Confuses Civics with Politics

The ruling class has come to see the mainstream as nettlesome at times but largely irrelevant as a political force. We are the backbone that supports the body politic; they are the muscles that decide where the body politic will go. We work, pay our taxes, and vote. And after we vote, we go back to work and hope that those in power will do the right thing.

We have trusted the dogs of the political class to guard our lunch, and they have eaten it.

Mainstream Americans play by the rules, both the rules of civics and the rules of polite behavior. In fact, following the rules is part of our character, and that comes from our Judeo-Christian worldview. And we trust others to do the same. But it has become obvious that we have put too much faith in elections and not enough in what happens between elections. We have put too much faith in the actions of elected officials and not enough in the actions of mainstream Americans in our families, in our communities, and in public politics.

The American mainstream confuses "civics" with "politics." Mainstream Americans know our civics; we understand the way the system is set up on paper. We know that government is supposed to be limited by the Constitution. We understand the checks and balances that were designed into the structure of our government to make it difficult for those with an agenda to force that agenda on the rest of us. We know our rights as they appear in the Constitution, and we know our responsibilities as citizens. We know that voting is *supposed* to give us the means to corral any government that steps outside of its constitutional bounds.

But politics is not the same as civics. Civics tells us how things *should* be; politics decides how things *will* be. Mainstream America brings *Robert's Rules of Order* to a political street fight, and we are losing our country as a result.

Elections may change the names on the doors in elected offices, but elections only affect formal power, not the power that lies within the cultural institutions. And power is what politics is all about. Not the common good, not the will of the people, not the Constitution; politics is about getting and using power to decide what will be done and how.

Certainly formal power rests in elected office, but cultural institutions have the power to make or break those in elected office, and the mainstream has lost those cultural institutions. Winning elections will accomplish little until we understand how power works, not only in the formal institutions of government but also in the culture on which those institutions rest.

In Politics, Good Citizens Make Great Losers

Mainstream Americans, even those we sometimes put in elected office, are babes in the woods in the world of power politics. Living our own lives and leaving others largely free to do the same is a defining characteristic of the mainstream. We count on the electoral process as it appears in the civics books to reflect our wishes, and our political involvement usually ends when we walk out of the voting booth. The left knows that we will vote and then go back to work like good citizens.

In fact, they count on it.

BULLY PULPITS AND JUST PLAIN BULLIES

Our elections, those sacred rituals of American politics, seem to have little effect on the direction in which the country moves. Even when the mainstream throws the left out of *office*, as we did in 1994 and 2000, we never seem to throw them out of *power*. We may slow their advance, but we never seem to take back any of the constitutional ground that we have lost. Government grows and liberty shrinks, regardless of who wins elections.

Leftists understand that elections are just the consolation prize of politics. The brass ring is control of the cultural institutions. When mainstream Americans win electoral landslides, the news and educational institutions ring with calls for the newcomers to "work together" with the left. "Compromise" is presented as the mature, responsible, and even American thing to do. They hint darkly at the "extremist" views of the newcomers.

When the left wins elections, on the other hand, those same institutions call for the losers to get out of the way and "listen to the voice of the people." Change has a positive spin when the change moves the country to the left and a negative spin when it moves us to the right.

Theodore Roosevelt called the presidency a "bully pulpit," but the real bully pulpit is the one that decides what questions the president will answer at a news conference, which questions will not be asked, and whether to run the flattering picture or the odd-looking one on the cover of a magazine. Whether the president or any elected official is presented as hero or villain, as brilliant or a bumbling incompetent, is decided throughout the institutions of news, education, and entertainment. Franklin Roosevelt's status as a hero for ending the Great Depression is a pure fiction invented by leftists in the educational institutions, but millions of American children have learned that fiction as fact.

Mainstream Americans are the summer tourists of politics, and liberals are the locals. For mainstreamers, politics is seasonal, revolving around the election cycle. We go home afterward, just like we go home after summer vacation. The left, on the other hand, stays behind in the institutions of power. They push their political agenda in the educational, news, and entertainment institutions, while we go home and push the lawnmower.

When leftists are in formal power, they fight aggressively to push their agenda, and the cultural institutions provide air cover, as they did during the debates on the bailouts and Obamacare. When the mainstream is in formal power, the cultural institutions become a fifth column of political snipers and saboteurs.

Just as a liberating army first seizes the means of communication, mainstream America will have to take back the cultural institutions that we have lost, the educational, news, and entertainment institutions that define the heroes and villains of our national politics. Only then will mainstream electoral victories be presented to the voters not as attempts to "turn back the clock," nor as setbacks in social progress, but as attempts to regain our constitutional republic from the left.

It took decades to lose those institutions, and it will take decades to win them back. But we do not have decades to turn America in a more sane direction, so this book will emphasize tactics that weaken the *impact* of those institutions even while they are controlled by the left.

But control of the cultural institutions—the bully pulpits of news, education, and entertainment—is only one way that liberals control the political narrative. In addition to controlling the bully pulpits, liberals can be just plain bullies.

THE SCHOOLYARD BULLIES OF POLITICS

Leftists do not prevail by making their case to the American people, at least in the sense of presenting a reasoned argument with supporting evidence. They make no effort to convince the American people that spending money we don't have or taxing the productive sector of the economy is sound fiscal policy. No liberal politician has yet demonstrated how adding to the tax burden of the productive sector of the economy will lead to economic prosperity. Hardcore liberals do not even attempt to justify their protection of free-speech rights for radical leftist professors while trying to shut down conservative talk show hosts. Nor do they attempt to offer rational explanations of how groping granny in airport security will keep Islamic terrorists off our airliners.

Leftists cannot defend the indefensible, so one of their tactics is to get their way by bullying. Accusations, name-calling, lies, demands, threats of lawsuits, and even intimations of violence—from left-wing race hustlers to union thugs, leftists all too often resemble those of the schoolyard bully.

As just one case in point, note that government employee unions do not even attempt to argue that union demands will benefit the public at large in any way, that their demands are fair, or even that their demands are realistic in the midst of the worst economy since the Great Depression. Instead, their message is as simple as that of the schoolyard bully: "Gimme what I want or else!"[7]

How do we make sense of such tactics?

SHINING LIGHT ON THE DARKNESS

In recent years, several writers have shed important light on the psychology of the left, describing it variously as a mental disorder,[8] a problem in emotional development,[9] and a form of mob psychology.[10] These works view liberalism from different perspectives, but a consistent picture seems to be emerging, one that can help mainstream Americans to more fully understand what we are up against and why our traditional methods of dealing with the left have failed so miserably.

In essence, these works have shattered the myth that hardcore liberals share the mainstream's fundamental goals of a prosperous and just America, differing from the rest of us only in the methods used to reach those goals. It is becoming apparent that, in order to break the left's grip on political power, the mainstream will have to fundamentally change our thinking about leftists as well as the tactics we use in dealing with them.

WORLDVIEW AND CHARACTER DIFFERENCES

In this book, we will present our own assessment of militant liberalism as a rejection of the Judeo-Christian worldview on which America was founded and also as a character trait defined by insatiable craving for power. We will argue that both are necessary to produce hardcore leftists, and that understanding both is essential to finding more effective tactics for dealing with them. This approach allows us to draw the critical distinction between the true leftist hardliners and those liberal voters who are merely uninformed or misinformed. That distinction will be essential to the strategy and tactics we offer in this book.

But, important though it is for the mainstream to understand the nature of the leftists who dominate our culture and who often resort to bullying to get their way, we also need to answer a sobering question, one that no one seems to have asked thus far: Why have mainstream Americans allowed ourselves to be outflanked in the cultural institutions and even bullied by the left-wing fringe? After all, we vastly outnumber the far left; only about 20 percent of the electorate identifies themselves as liberal.

One bully cannot terrorize an entire playground, and 20 percent of the population cannot impose their views and policies on the rest of us—unless the majority allows them to do so.

We Take the High Road and They Take the Low Road

If anyone raises a ruckus about a school's budget, it is the left-wing teachers' union, not the mainstream taxpayers, even though we are the ones who actually fund that budget. Government unions take to the streets and occupy state capitals whenever mainstream officials try to bring sanity to state spending, as we saw in Wisconsin during the summer of 2011.

But for decades the taxpayers have had no such organized force. We've been too busy working to pay the bills. We vote, and then we hope that our elected officials will do the right thing.

And the odd thing about that is, just as the better-behaved children on the playground outnumber the bully, mainstream America outnumbers the political bullies on our left. Our sheer numerical advantage should tell us that we could stop liberal bullying at any time, if we were willing to do so. But, like the well-behaved children on the playground, mainstream Americans just want to get along with others and take care of our responsibilities. We play by the rules, and the bullies know it.

Leftists Use Our Maturity Against Us

Mainstream Americans don't have the stomach for the unpleasantness of confrontation with the political bullies of the left for two reasons. One is that we have learned more mature ways of handling our differences, and those mature ways work fine when we have differences with other mainstream Americans who share our basic worldview and character traits. The problem is that those mature ways of handling differences—explaining, reasoning, offering evidence, appealing to fairness—are totally ineffective when dealing with the radical left.

The other reason we have failed to stop liberal bullying is that social unpleasantness triggers a deep discomfort in many mainstream Americans, precisely because we have been raised to be good citizens. The hardcore left seems to thrive on emotional and social strife; mainstream Americans thrive on order and a reasonable degree of harmony. It is becoming evident that leftists see our maturity and our peace-loving nature as weaknesses that they can exploit to dominate us. And that is why a small number of hardcore leftists have almost destroyed the freest and most prosperous country that ever existed.

Well before Barack Obama issued his infamous call for his followers to "get in their faces" when people did not toe the left-wing line, liberals have resorted to name-calling, wild accusations, and lying about the intentions of the mainstream as a way of making us back down.[11] And it has usually worked.

The rules of good citizenship that we learned as children work well when we are dealing with others who operate by the same rules. But few experiences in life have prepared the mainstream's good citizens for dealing with leftists who "get in our faces." Their accusations, demands, insinuations, and name-calling trigger discomfort and confusion. Too often, we fall back on habits such as explaining, reasoning, offering evidence, and—all too often—compromising in order to restore the peace.

Those habits work with others who play by the same rules and who want peace and harmony with us. The problem is that leftists don't play by the same rules, and they don't want peace and harmony.

Leftists just want power.

WE HAVE BEEN FIGHTING THE WRONG FIGHT

How many times have you seen a mainstream citizen on television trying to defend against the charge that the Tea Party is racist or that talk radio somehow causes mass shootings? How many times have you heard some mainstream American pointing out that many of the Tea Party's political favorites are black conservatives, that there is not a shred of video evidence of racism in Tea Party rallies, that the only violence at a Tea Party rally occurred when liberal bullies beat up a black vendor?[12]

How many times have you heard mainstream Americans explaining that this or that mass shooter had a psychiatric history, or that the shooter never listened to talk radio?

How many times have you been the one making those or similar arguments? How many times have you tried to explain to some leftist that catastrophic spending will hurt the very people the leftists claim to care about, or that raising taxes on employers will make unemployment even worse?

And what good has it done?

We have written this book so that mainstream Americans can understand the worldview and the character of the far left, because only then does it become clear why our traditional methods of dealing with leftists have been totally ineffective. Only then will the need for the strategies and tactics presented in this book become evident.

Before we can equip the sleeping giant for the struggle ahead of us, however, we need to *wake* that sleeping giant. And as it turns out, Obama, Reid, and Pelosi may have done that for us.

THE LEFT BLOWS THEIR COVER

Gradual erosion has been a longtime component of the far left's strategy to sink the United States into the bog of statism. But with the election of 2008, the gradual erosion of our liberty gave way to a tsunami of blatantly socialist and unpopular policies. Obama's palace of "czars" was filled with America-hating radicals who openly disdain and despise the American mainstream and our Judeo-Christian values, and who openly pushed a Marxist agenda.

This time, even their allies in the news and educational systems could not provide cover for the left's agenda. No one could spin the new regime's arrogance and abuse of power as just different ideas about how to preserve and protect America. The left's cover was blown. Mainstream America began to reach the inescapable conclusion that we are in a political struggle not with people who share our goals of a free and prosperous America but whose methods differ from ours, but that we are in a struggle with people who want to radically transform America into a top-down oligarchy run by a leftist elite.

Maybe the success of their strategy of gradualism had made the left overly confident by the time of the 2008 election. After all, they have gotten bolder and bolder since the radical 1960s, and nothing had stopped them. Or possibly—indeed, hopefully—the far left underestimated the intelligence and backbone of normal Americans. In any case, the true agenda of the far left was exposed after 2008, and millions of mainstream Americans were stunned by what they saw.

THE GIANT AWAKENS

Like the Japanese attack on Pearl Harbor, the left's strategy in 2008 was a sneak attack. They came in under a fog of rhetoric about "hope" and "change," and they caught the mainstream sleeping.

And, like the Japanese navy after Pearl Harbor, the left knows that they have to do irreparable damage to the free enterprise system in a short time if they are to set the stage for a socialist system. They know that they have awakened the sleeping giant of the American mainstream and "filled him with a terrible resolve." They know they cannot prevail against our numbers *if we are willing to give them a protracted struggle.*

Just as America's victory at the Battle of Midway spoiled the Japanese strategy of winning an overwhelming victory early in the war and gave us time to mobilize our industrial might, the mainstream's stunning victory in the 2010 election may not have won the war, but it bought time for us to mobilize.

WHAT DO WE DO NOW?

The sleeping giant is finally awake, and many in the political mainstream are joining the fight for America's future. But unlike the radical left, mainstream Americans are not political animals. Grassroots movements like the Tea Party might mobilize us, but we are not seasoned activists. We have to be equipped and trained for the protracted struggle. Waking the giant was the first step. But getting into the political fray will require a major change in mainstream thinking and actions. We will need a new political strategy and far more effective tactics.

After all, the mainstream voters of today are the schoolyard's well-behaved children of yesterday. Once we realize that we cannot appease the bully by giving him our lunch money—and our spending crisis combined with angry liberal demands for more spending has made that clear—we have to find another way to deal with the problem.

But how do we turn our mainstream good citizens into seasoned, hard-hitting political activists? We have written this book as a handbook for that purpose.

THREE QUESTIONS

We have organized this book around three questions to help us understand liberal strategies and tactics, the kind of people who could conceive of those strategies and condone those tactics, and why our response must be radically different than it has been in the past.

1. *How has the liberal minority forced their agenda through our government, our schools and universities, the news media, entertainment, and even medicine and science?*

We will describe the liberals' Long March through these cultural institutions, and we will go into detail about the most common liberal tactics for bullying anyone who gets in their way.

2. *How are liberals different from those in the mainstream?*

We will look at what kind of people would use tactics such as those used by the hardcore left. We will describe the roots of the liberal worldview and also provide insights into character traits that combine to produce the hardcore leftist. Understanding the worldview and the character of this kind of person will be critical for learning to use the new and more effective tactics we cover in this book.

3. *How does the political mainstream need to change our tactics if we are to regain and protect our freedom?*

We will offer strategies and tactics for breaking the momentum of the left's advance, turning liberal assaults against them, and seizing control of the nation's political discourse.

When you finish that section, you will be prepared to handle common liberal tactics up to and including the notorious race card.

But before we answer those questions, we need to clarify how liberals ever win elections when they comprise at most 20 percent of the electorate, compared to self-identified conservatives, who comprise 40 percent.

LIBERAL SPOTTING

Unless we specify otherwise, when we mention liberals in this book, we are talking about hardcore liberals, those true-believing leftists who are most dangerous to a constitutional republic. They do not have the votes to win elections, so they depend on people who are uninformed and misinformed to help them reach an electoral majority. The strategy and tools in this book are designed to reach the uninformed and misinformed people who give the radical left their power. By using these tools, you will also engage and mobilize the conservative base.

The techniques that we cover in this book require an awareness of your audience. There is probably nothing you can do to convince a hardened leftist that he is wrong. But even when dealing directly with a hardened leftist, say, in a debate for a school board position or at a town hall meeting, your handling of the leftist will still influence the uninformed and misinformed voters who hear the exchange. As we will demonstrate, you want to both discredit the leftist (for several reasons that will become clear) and educate the other listeners. However, if your audience is only one person, like your daughter who has just come home from college spouting liberal rhetoric, you will not need the same hard-hitting tools that you would use in debating the hardened leftist, and instead you can focus on an educational approach.

The principles and methods we cover will apply across a range of situations, but you will need to adapt them to your audience. So let's look briefly at the different types of audiences.

Liberal hardliners are able to occasionally win elections because they hoodwink people who are uninformed and misinformed. As we will see, the hardliners are the intellectual descendants of Nietzsche, Marx, and others who rejected the Judeo-Christian worldview. And it is the rejection of that worldview that leads them to the destructive and amoral tactics that they use.

You are unlikely to convert a hardened leftist, so your goal with them will be twofold: to discredit their position for the benefit of others who are present and to sap their political confidence. Both goals are critical if we are to take back our culture, and we will cover methods for doing so in later chapters.

Unlike the hardcore leftist, the uninformed and misinformed share many of the values of the mainstream, and they are not committed disciples of Marx or Alinsky. When they vote for liberal politicians and give the hardcore left an electoral victory, the damage they do is accidental rather than malicious. They know not what they do.

The *uninformed* are typically not that interested in politics; they vote with the prevailing political wind. If they are doing well personally, they vote for the party in power. If they are having a hard time, they vote for the other guy. During the 2008 election, Obama looked cool, while McCain looked boring and confused about what he believed. The uninformed vote went to Obama that year.

To understand the *misinformed*, think of college students who have been raised in mainstream homes, who have many mainstream values, yet who come home from college spouting trendy liberal rhetoric. Think of your neighbors who work hard, go to church, and seem to be good citizens, but fall for the leftist promise of "abundance for all." If these folks vote, they probably vote for the liberal candidate because they have been immersed in the idea that liberals are sophisticated and smart, whereas conservatives are ignorant.

But there is a huge difference between liberal hardliners and people who vote for liberals because they have been misinformed. When misinformed voters talk about the need for tolerance, diversity, helping the poor, caring for the environment, and the importance of education, they really mean it. That is the critical difference between misinformed liberal voters and the liberal hardliners who run the political show.

Liberal hardliners use sweet rhetoric merely as a political tactic. The rhetoric is designed to hoodwink the uninformed and misinformed. The methods in this book are designed to expose the reality behind the rhetoric and to educate the uninformed and misinformed.

Our goal is to restore our constitutional republic. But when the house is on fire, that's no time to debate the finer points of interior decorating. Though this book is written from a conservative point of view, we will deliberately gloss over differences between libertarian and traditional conservatives, free-traders and economic nationalists, and others who want to restore legitimate constitutional government. Until mainstream Americans pull our country back from the brink of collapse, our rule needs to be "I have no enemies to the right of me." People to the right of you might not always believe what you believe, but neither will they take away your liberty.

If we cannot stop and reverse the Long March of the radical left, then the differences among the different members of the mainstream won't matter. The radical left will have won. The American dream will be dead. We will have become what liberals have long wanted us to become: subjects of their government and not citizens of a republic.

2

WHAT AILS US

How has the liberal minority forced their agenda through our government, our schools and universities, the news media, entertainment, and even medicine and science?

MARXISM THROUGH CULTURAL REVOLUTION

Though American culture, and consequently our system of government, is unquestionably founded upon the Judeo-Christian worldview, there has been a concerted effort for over one hundred years to undermine our Judeo-Christian culture as a means of seizing political power for the far left.

This subversion of our culture has not been a cloak-and-dagger conspiracy with passwords and secret handshakes. The agents of subversion did not meet in shadowed alleys and speak in hushed tones for fear of detection. Instead, it has been a political movement openly promoted by leftist intellectuals in Europe and then adopted and carried out by a hardcore leftist minority in the United States. They spoke openly in lecture halls to their idealistic but naïve students, and they wrote of their ideas in articles and books for anyone to read.

Their movement was not completely unified; there were debates and differences among those intellectuals about theories and methods. What they had in common, however, was a rejection of the Judeo-Christian worldview and a belief that history would move us inexorably toward a socialist state. America's constitutional republic, with its grounding in Judeo-Christian values, was destined for the trash bin of history.[13]

A Long March, Not a Conspiracy

In classical Marxist theory, the workers of the world would unite and throw off the chains of the capitalist system. But, as is often the case with leftist intellectual ideas, reality does not comply with the demands of the theory. Russia, with its agrarian economy and its social classes sharply divided between the wealthy and the peasantry, was ripe for the hollow promises of communism. But Russia turned out to be the exception.

Classical Marxists believed that capitalism would result in wealth for the owners of the means of production and poverty for workers. Instead, capitalism raised the standard of living of both owners and workers. Those more prosperous countries were not as receptive to the idea of violent revolution to bring about the communist utopia. The larger and more comfortable the working and middle classes became, the harder it was to sell the idea of violently overthrowing the existing structure. Marxist theorists began to recognize that real political power rested in many ways upon the culture of the country, and that the path to formal political power lay in eroding the cultural foundations of Western civilization. As it turned out, that strategy proved far more successful than one of violent revolution.

Don't Ask a Fish

There is an old proverb that says, "If you want to understand water, don't ask a fish." To the fish, water is just the way things are. Because they are immersed in it, it is normal to them. Nothing about water is remarkable to the fish. The same principle applies to culture and its effect on our way of thinking about the world.[14]

As we grow up, we absorb the ways of looking at the world and the rules for behaving without giving them much thought. Cultural norms are "just the way we do things around here." We don't remember the precise moment that we learned, for example, to speak in hushed tones at a funeral or to shake hands when we meet someone. It's just what people do. We don't *convert* to those habits and the values behind them, we just absorb them. They are part of the world in which we swim.

Many of our political values are learned the same way as we learn other cultural habits. Earlier generations of Americans learned that America is good just as effortlessly as we learned to wait to be seated in some restaurants and to seat ourselves in others. We learned that people get married before they have children as easily as we learned to cover our mouths and to say "excuse me" when we sneeze. We learned that men are responsible for providing for the children that they father, and we learned that we work for what we get. We learned a political philosophy without ever thinking about it, just as we learned that we drive on the right in America.

There was no argument about these customs and practices; there was no debate. Through constant exposure, these customs and practices were just absorbed. And we did not challenge these beliefs and practices, because they were not presented to us as options; they were not new ideas we would have to choose to embrace or reject.

Often, it is only when we are exposed to beliefs and practices in other cultures that we realize just how much our cultural assumptions shape us. Angry Americans might give the "middle-finger salute" to a politician we dislike, but the thought of waving our shoes at an unpopular politician seems as bizarre to us as it seems normal in other parts of the world. Culture shapes what we notice, what we assume, and what we believe, and we don't even know it's happening.

POLLUTING THE CULTURAL POND

The cultural Marxists figured out how to mount an assault on America that even our powerful military could not repel. They knew that if Americans grow up absorbing habits of independence and personal responsibility, then those pushing the leftist agenda would encounter cultural resistance at every turn.

But if we could be made to grow up without moral constraints, we would lack the moral basis for evaluating the actions of those in power. If we could grow up absorbing the habits of dependency and blame, assuming that government has a role in everything we do, then an amoral government that fosters dependency and blame, one that involves itself in every aspect of our lives, would seem perfectly normal. And any politicians who spoke of personal responsibility would seem out of touch with the way things really are.

The cultural Marxists realized that the easiest path to power ran through the cultural institutions that teach us how to think about things and how to behave, the very institutions that shape our character. They understood that public schools could immerse students in assumptions and beliefs through textbooks, curriculum, and the influence of teachers. They understood that news media shape our understanding of politics by what gets omitted, what gets covered, and how things get covered. Entertainment, unions, churches, professional associations, and charitable organizations could all be used to gradually embed Marxist ideas in popular culture.

When the revolution occurs through gradual cultural change, it is not necessary to convert people to Marxism. It is not necessary to make the case that an all-powerful government can run our lives better than we can. For example, it is not necessary to convince anyone that the purpose of taxation is to redistribute earnings rather than simply to provide funding for necessary functions of government. You just start with a small progressive income tax that affects only the most successful people in society. Once the Marxist idea of a progressive tax becomes accepted, you ramp it up little by little. Eventually, the idea that the rich should pay more is embedded in the culture, and few people question the implications of a government that can redistribute the fruits of our labors. There is no honest discussion of the risks, the hard work, investment of time and resources, and personal sacrifices behind those earnings; to do so would undermine the assumption that successful people should pay a heavier price for their success.

All that is necessary is to embed Marxist thinking little by little in the institutions of culture. The government will fall to the leftist agenda without a shot being fired.

Those driving their leftist agenda have no need to make the case that socialism is fair or that it works well in practice, and there is no opportunity for those on the receiving end of the dogma to reflect, accept, or reject leftist propositions. Those propositions are not presented as propositions for consideration. Like water to a fish, socialist ideas look normal to people who have been surrounded by those ideas from childhood.

Subverting Children First

It's easy to see why the early Marxist intellectuals viewed our educational system as a prime target. In public school, our children learn that we do not pray or mention God in public, and they do not ask why. Or if they do ask why, those in positions of authority tell them that religion is a private matter. Children don't ask why, if religion is a private matter, they are taught to be sensitive to the practices of Muslims but not of Christians. They don't know to ask. It's just the way things are.

Children learn that it is only fair that more successful people should pay more in taxes because that view is not presented to them as one option among many; the underlying assumptions are not discussed. That view is presented as a given, as just the way things are. Children do not ask how long "the rich" had to work and how much hardship they endured before they became rich, and they do not ask how many people are employed by those "rich" people, because children do not know to ask. And educational institutions run by leftists do not provide that perspective.

Children do not know enough to ask why they are not studying the Constitution and the Federalist Papers, and they cannot recognize propaganda as such when they hear a leftist version of our history. They have no way of knowing what has been distorted or left out altogether. If those students hear and absorb, for example, the myth that Roosevelt's massive expansion of government put an end to the Great Depression, then "big government is good for us" becomes the cultural norm. They have no way of knowing that Roosevelt's policies actually *prolonged* the Great Depression, and as adult voters they will not understand why government "stimulus" spending only worsens a bad economy.

I'M NOT A MARXIST, BUT I VOTE LIKE ONE

There is no one point in a cultural revolution at which people become convinced that the left has better ideas or at which people are "converted" to the leftist worldview. When the revolution occurs through slow cultural change, no one has to actually *become* a Marxist. The process is more one of immersion than one of conversion. We soak up the rules of our culture; we do not think about them, debate them, or make a conscious choice about adopting them. The victims do not even see it happening, especially when the victims are children and the ones they learn from are teachers.

It is essential to realize that many of the teachers, newscasters, and others who do their jobs from a Marxist worldview in all likelihood would not think of themselves as Marxists. They were simply taught by people who were taught by people who were taught by people who were Marxists, or who were leftists friendly to Marxist ideas.

That is the power of the cultural institutions. That is how the radical left's 20 percent ensures that enough uninformed and misinformed voters give them occasional victories at the polls.

THREE TARGETS: FAMILY, COUNTRY, AND GOD

It also became evident to the cultural Marxists that the traditional family, with its emphasis on parental authority as the means of providing for the upkeep and moral training of children, did not fit well with the notion of an all-powerful central government. When Hillary Clinton likened marriage to the master–slave relationship in one of her college writings, she reflected the influence of these neo-Marxist theorists.[15]

Another cultural barrier to Marxist rule was nationalism. As became evident during World War I, the working class that provided most of the soldiers felt more loyalty to their fellow countrymen of all social classes than to some internationalist workers' revolt. Marxist intellectuals realized that the workers of the world were not joining together to throw off their supposed chains; they were joining with their fellow countrymen of all social classes to fight their country's enemies.

But nationalism and patriotism get in the way of the internationalist plans of the radical left. The current leftist insistence that the United States surrender its sovereignty and bow to the wishes of the United Nations, their disdain for Fourth of July celebrations, and their preference for open borders are right in line with the early Marxist push to eliminate nationhood as a barrier to Marxist rule.

Yet another cultural barrier to the leftist agenda was the role played by traditional religion. The very notion of a power higher than political power, the teaching of absolute standards of right and wrong, and the belief that life on this planet is only the beginning of something bigger, all worked against the atheistic materialism of the Marxist worldview. The left's hostility to any expression of Judeo-Christian morality, regardless of how nondenominational it may be, suggests that it is not the establishment of a state religion that so threatens them—it is the cultural acceptance of power beyond that of government.[16]

THE LONG MARCH BEGINS

It was this recognition of the power of culture, of culture as the underpinnings of formal political power, that ignited the interest of the leftist theorists at the Frankfurt School in Germany and, later, at the New School for Social Research in New York. Among others, Max Horkheimer, Theodor Adorno, Antonio Gramsci, Georg Lukacs, and Herbert Marcuse—names unfamiliar to most Americans today—became household names among earlier generations of left-wing activists. What emerged from their work was a new brand of Marxist theory, one that preached the slow, piecemeal takeover of the institutions of a nation's culture as the path to eventual control of the formal reins of government.[17]

The "long march through the institutions," a phrase coined by Gramsci, was presented as a slower but surer alternative to the far riskier business of violent revolution. Such an approach could occur right under the noses of the mainstream, which is an important consideration, given that the mainstream would have ridden the Marxists out of town on a rail if their intentions had been obvious.

TRICKLE-DOWN LIBERALISM

Most people have little interest in the economic theories and philosophical debates that rage within the halls of the universities. But trendy ideas in universities eventually filter down to other institutions. People who couldn't care less about the theories of the cultural Marxists still send their children to school, and most people get their news from newspapers, radio, and television. Most people also enjoy an occasional play, movie, or sitcom. It was through these cultural institutions that the worldview friendly to Marxism would be conveyed, not all at once, but through a gradual shift in the assumptions and values that were embedded in the news, in the heroes and villains of the stories, and in the textbooks.

A popular theme among the cultural leftists was the notion that truth and reality are socially constructed and not absolutes. This kind of relativistic thinking was popular among the Frankfurt School writers, and in retrospect, it's easy to see why. When there are no fixed reference points of truth or reality, then anything goes.

Think about the consequences of labeling all morals as just social habits with no inherent value. The skyrocketing illegitimacy rate since the cultural revolution of the sixties, especially in the black community, has had devastating consequences for everyone except the leftist politicians whose policies foster that illegitimacy and who rake in the votes on election day.[18] But anyone who raises the issue is accused by liberals of imposing an arbitrary definition of family on others.

As the left loves to say, "who are we to say" what a man should do when he fathers a child? The idea of truth and morality as socially constructed serves the left's purpose of undermining traditional values that get in the way of the Long March. When the body's antibodies are weakened, an infection can grow with less resistance. The same principle applies when a culture's antibodies—its presuppositions and values—are weakened.

Centuries of accumulated wisdom, the lessons learned by trial and error across generations and handed down as presuppositions and values, can be erased with a simple "Who are we to say? . . ." For leftist intellectuals, every aspect of Western culture was subjected to just that kind of skeptical challenge.

THE LEFTIST WORLDVIEW SPREADS

Students immersed in left-wing dogma in schools then fan out into journalism, entertainment, pulpits, and other cultural institutions and, eventually, into the voting booths of the nation.

As a way of forcing the leftist agenda on an unsuspecting and even unwilling majority, the Long March approach has succeeded in undermining the culture and rights of mainstream Americans just as dripping water eventually erodes a rock. The result has been domination by leftist thinking and actions in universities, public schools, old media, entertainment, nonprofits, the career bureaucracy, and even some larger corporations that are vulnerable to political pressure. Liberal dominance in these institutions, especially news and education, has been documented extensively.[19]

It is noteworthy that our Founding Fathers also understood the foundational role of culture as illustrated by John Adams' statement that "Our Constitution was made only for a moral and religious people. It is wholly inadequate to the government of any other." These words clearly and simply make the case that our original system of government, with its protection for liberty and the separation of governmental powers, rested on the moral and religious foundations of our culture.

The fact that, after the 2008 election, leftist teachers led students in psalms of praise to Obama and not to John Adams tells us which side is winning the culture war.[20]

But how about the formal machinery of government, where laws and policies are actually made? Certainly the left wins some elections and seizes governmental power at times, but at other times they are thrown out on their collectivist ears, or at least they appear to be. So what about those times that mainstream candidates win elections and have their hands on the machinery of power? Wouldn't those times of mainstream resurgence provide a critical check and balance on the influence of the far left? Wouldn't the proverbial pendulum swing back toward the will of the mainstream? After all, the left makes up only a small percentage of the population, so it seems reasonable that they would have difficulty imposing their agenda when the mainstream has far greater numbers at the polls.

GOVERNMENT IS ONLY THE TIP OF THE POWER ICEBERG

The unfortunate reality is that the left only appears to lose power when they lose elections. In the grand scheme of politics, elections only affect the visible and formal aspects of power. Winning elections is certainly important, but winning an election is vastly different from driving a political agenda. As the cultural Marxists realized, political power is like an iceberg, and the formal machinery of government is only the visible tip of that iceberg. The bulk of the power in the country is hidden beneath the surface, in the institutions of culture that shape the day-to-day assumptions and interpretations of the political world.

When the mainstream wins an election and sits atop the power iceberg, the left remains in full control of the far larger chunk beneath the surface. Liberal dominance of America's cultural institutions—especially the news media and education—means that they can actively undermine the influence of the mainstream elected officials, and they can join forces with leftist officials to shape the agenda when they are in power.

Seizing the institutions of culture by way of the Long March is a slower process than violent revolution, but it allows the takeover of a country to happen *right under the noses of the mainstream.* The institutions—including the alphabet soup of associations, committees, nonprofits, governmental bureaucracies, and pressure groups—set the political priorities. It is in these institutions that the national agenda emerges and the terms of political discussion are defined and shaped. They select and prepare the playing field where the elections will be held and the policy battles will be fought, regardless of who wins the elections. And though they are a minority of the population at large, the left owns most of these institutions lock, stock, and barrel.

Because they control the cultural institutions, the left controls the political "narrative," as the story told in our national discourse is often described. Liberals in the news media and classrooms are in positions to present liberal politicians as heroes and mainstream politicians as villains. They present liberals as experts and mainstreamers as crackpots. Obama's claim that he had campaigned in fifty-seven states with only one to go was ignored by the media because they wanted to portray Obama as brilliant. Sarah Palin was ridiculed as a simpleton for pointing out the fact that her state of Alaska shares a border with

Russia. The left claims that the science is "settled" on global warming and Darwinism while mocking skeptics as "global warming deniers" and God-and-guns Bible thumpers.

That's how, even after mainstream Americans took the left to the woodshed in the 2010 election, our new representatives started out on the defensive. From day one after the election results were in, the left fell back into its decades-old tactics. They shouted the old narrative through the cultural institutions that the new representatives of the mainstream wanted to push Granny off a cliff, that they were going to shut down the government, and that they were going to default on the debt that the left had run up.

And what was the sin of the new representatives to deserve such acrimony? That they wanted to get control of the liberal spending that had given our children a $15 trillion debt. If the news media had even the remotest interest in objectivity, they would have focused attention on the *causes* of the economic crisis, such as the damage done to the mortgage market by liberal pressure to make loans based on political criteria instead of business criteria, or the political payoffs in the left's $800 billion "stimulus" package, or the money-laundering schemes in which liberal politicians funnel money to their huge contributors, such as unions, who then return the favor with political contributions. How much easier would it have been to avoid the economic crisis in the first place if the news had been presented by objective professionals instead of by liberal operatives? Federal spending and corruption would have been defined as a problem long before the debt reached such catastrophic levels, and politicians who advocated more spending and borrowing would have been presented to the public as irresponsible.

Such media bias does not affect the 40 percent of us who define ourselves as conservatives, and the 20 percent who define themselves as liberal probably don't believe much of their own rhetoric anyway. But it can easily sway the opinions of the uninformed and misinformed, even those who share much of the moral worldview and character traits of the mainstream.

THE POLITICAL POWER OF CULTURE

Because we "swim" in culture just as fish swim in water, it might be hard to realize just how much damage the left has done through their dominance in these institutions. Biased news reports and ridicule of mainstream Americans just seem normal.

To fully grasp the extent of the left's dominance and the damage they have done, it might be helpful to imagine an America in which mainstream values permeated our cultural institutions.

IMAGINE MAINSTREAM NEWS AND SCHOOLS; IT'S EASY IF YOU TRY . . .

Let's try a thought experiment. Imagine that God performed an overnight miracle and converted everyone in our educational system, news media, and other cultural institutions into mainstream Americans. Imagine that these new mainstreamers woke up the next day alarmed at the erosion of our Constitution and the arrogance and corruption of our government. If they were to use their power to try to restore legitimate constitutional government, what effect would that have on those holding the formal reins of government? How long would it take?

On day one of the Great Awakening, teachers would begin to convey to their students the superiority of liberty and free enterprise. Students would begin to hear that free enterprise is more efficient and humane than any other economic system. Students would learn about the horrors brought about by big government in the twentieth century, when over 100 million citizens died at the hands of left-wing governments, and those students would be held accountable for learning and remembering the lessons of those horrors.

If leftist politicians were in the headlines calling for "stimulus spending" to deal with the debt crisis, students would be asked by their teachers, with a wink and a nod, whether a family that cannot pay its credit card bill should be given another credit card. Critical-thinking exercises would focus on the impact of higher taxes on job creation. Pop quizzes would follow to ensure retention.

For Black History Month, students would read about Justice Clarence Thomas as a role model. Books by Dr. Walter Williams and Dr. Thomas Sowell would be required to ensure that our children learned fundamental principles of economics and the danger of governmental meddling in economic decisions. The writings of Frederick Douglass would be familiar fare.

Now imagine that, within a few months of the Great Awakening, those students heard some community organizer from the notoriously corrupt Chicago political machine saying that he just wants to "spread the wealth around." Their response would be, "Sounds like a commie to me! Forget this guy." Instead of swooning in awe, America's youth would give this leftist a collective raspberry under the approving smiles of their teachers. It would be very uncool to be a leftist within just a few months of the Great Awakening.

Dream a little more with us and imagine a liberal politician facing a question like this in a news interview: "Exactly where in the Constitution do you find the authority for the government to take over the health care of working families?" Or this: "It appears that the labor unions would be the biggest beneficiaries of your proposed bailout. Just how much have you received in contributions from those unions?"

Uniformed and misinformed liberal voters would be confronted with a new perspective. That night, they would watch an hour-long special on the horrors of socialized medicine. They would hear reports of doctors in England prescribing water—yes, water—so that their patients wouldn't go thirsty in hospitals run by government bureaucrats.[21]

The language used in news reports would be very different because it would reflect very different values. Health care "reform" would become health care "takeover" on the evening news. "Stimulus bill" would become "controversial bailout" in newspaper headlines. Imagine leftist politicians with microphones in their faces and reporters shouting, "With working families already struggling under the weight of government that many believe to be spiraling out of control, how do you justify your plan to add to the tax burden of those families?"

Or maybe: "How do you justify the damage done to black families by your policies? How do you respond to charges that you don't care as long as you get elected? Sir, please answer the question." Can you visualize the news footage of the liberal politician pushing his hand in front of the camera lens and ducking into a limo to escape further questions?

Uninformed voters, those with little interest in politics, would pick up the idea that leftist politicians are definitely not the heroes of our national story. Voters misinformed by years of leftist propaganda would have their eyes opened to new information, new perspectives, and new questions. It would become very unsophisticated to vote liberal.

Try to suspend your disbelief for a moment longer. Imagine that this mainstream trend has spread through other cultural institutions. Maybe there would be a popular television sitcom with a wise mainstream president who outwits a bunch of laughable leftist opponents and journalists every week. Maybe one of the liberal characters—and we realize this is a stretch—would be a wealthy environmentalist who got rich from the global warming scam and who flies around in a private jet and lives in a tremendous mansion.

Another particularly ludicrous character might be the head of the Tolerance Task Force who loses her temper and screams intolerantly at anyone who disagrees with her. The Gucci shoes and designer suits of the Anti-Poverty League activist would become a standing joke around the country.

When viewers went to work the next morning, they would recount their favorite parts around the coffee machine, and laughter would echo down the hall. Leftist hypocrisy would be accepted as a cultural fact, and liberals would be turned into ludicrous caricatures, serving to provide humor to the mainstream.

Dream with us just a little longer. Imagine motion pictures in which the villains were multibillionaires pushing the global warming scam as a cover for a worldwide power grab, and the hero was a maverick scientist who exposed them. Or the villain was a thuggish union organizer in a factory and the hero a woman who stood up to the union. Or the villain was a corrupt left-wing president and the heroes two mainstream reporters whose work forced that president to resign.

In such a culture, it would be liberals instead of mainstream Americans who felt out of place. Liberals would feel outnumbered, isolated, as if they had to speak in hushed tones about their zany ideas. Their proclamations would lose the tone of moral superiority. Just as mainstreamers now feel the need to hedge our remarks with disclaimers like, "I'm not a racist, but I don't think affirmative action is fair," it would be liberals who walked on eggshells when expressing their views. Instead of "You have no right to force your religion down my throat and I'm going to stop you," liberals would feel social pressure to couch their remarks very carefully, as in, "I'm not an anti-Christian bigot, but I do have doubts about the public display of the Ten Commandments. Sometimes, just sometimes."

Now imagine that in such a culture an unknown community organizer with no supervisory experience and a background shrouded in mist decides that he should take over and run the health care system for three hundred million people. If he got any coverage at all, it would be on *America's Funniest Home Videos*.

We would have taken our country back—just as we have lost it—without a shot being fired.

That is the power of cultural institutions, and only by capturing these institutions will mainstream America have any lasting impact on our formal government.

Now Back to Living in an Occupied Country

Now let's get back to the reality of living in a country in which every major cultural institution is a soapbox for the leftist values of no more than 20 percent of the population.

The left dominates the news media, and news stories about homelessness increase under Republican presidents and disappear when a Democrat is in the Oval Office.[22] The unspoken message is clear: Homelessness is only a problem when Republicans are in office.

In the narrative pushed by the news and educational institutions, global warming suddenly becomes a crisis that can only be solved by more government and less liberty. People who question the science behind global warming are not hailed as mavericks or skeptics but are ridiculed as "global warming deniers."[23] You know, like "Holocaust deniers."

In the left's narrative, the invasion of the United States by illegal aliens becomes a story about xenophobia and racism among mainstream Americans, not about the integrity of our borders or the ability of our culture to assimilate millions of foreigners,[24] and most certainly not a story about voter fraud and those who benefit from it.

In reality, the Tea Party is a sign of life in mainstream America, a sign of hope that the mainstream giant has awakened. But the liberal media's narrative is about supposed racism and potential violence from the Tea Party.[25] Apparently community organizing is a good thing when liberals do it, but not when the community that organizes is the taxpaying community.

Such is the power of the cultural institutions. The European Marxists knew what they were doing. Mainstream Americans live like subjects in an occupied country.

WINNING ELECTIONS WILL NEVER BE ENOUGH

The election of Ronald Reagan in 1980 and the Republican victory in the US Senate appeared to signal a rebirth of common sense and resurgence of influence by a political mainstream that had suffered under Jimmy Carter's liberalism. Consider also the national election of 1994: In what appeared to be a tidal wave of rejection of the corruption and abuses of power by the 1960s radicals who came to Washington with the Clintons, Republicans seized both the Senate and the House for the first time in decades. They defeated Hillarycare and reformed welfare.

That certainly looks like the mainstream was in power. The system we read about in our civics books worked, didn't it? In these and other electoral defeats for liberals, the mainstream moved the political pendulum back toward our values and our way of thinking. Didn't we?

Nope. The leftist *advance* may have been slowed after mainstream electoral victories, or even stalled briefly, but they never *surrendered* an inch of the ground they had captured. The Department of Education—Jimmy Carter's political payoff to the teachers' unions—not only remained intact but also received more taxpayer money year after year to push the liberal agenda through textbooks and education policy. Regardless of who was at the tip of the political iceberg, textbooks morphed year after year into thinly disguised indoctrination tools.[26]

No federal department or bureaucracy has been eliminated under mainstream administrations, no matter how flagrant their abuse of power or how moronic and wasteful their policies. No leftist judges have been impeached and removed from power for substituting their own political biases for law.

Mainstream America will never save our country by winning elections as long as our opponents report on those elections, teach our children, and entertain the public.

What we read in the civics books will not save our republic.

BRILLIANT STRATEGY, NASTY TACTICS

The left's Long March strategy has proven to be a brilliant one. Because of their dominance of cultural institutions, liberals have a forum from which they can write the narrative, the terms of political debate. The left's virtual ownership of the news media, the schools, and other cultural institutions allows them to define the terms and questions of the nation's politics without even appearing to do so. The liberal minority has depicted the mainstream majority as outsiders in our own country.

But the left's ability to affect policy regardless of who sits in formal positions of power goes far beyond their ability to shape the terms of debate or to control access to information. Their dominance depends on a second and more disturbing factor: The left has a really nasty side, and they are willing to show it.

Liberals have learned that the bully usually gets his way, and liberals are willing to get loud, intimidating, and threatening. They are willing and eager to isolate, attack, and demolish anyone who resists their agenda. Anyone who proves inconvenient to them is met with vitriol and venomous attacks. Physical threats and even assaults upon anyone who disagrees with them are ever-present possibilities. But liberal bullying never becomes a news story, because the bullies and their allies run the newsrooms.

Finally, as we are about to see, the left's Long March through our institutions has succeeded because liberals understand the mainstream better than the mainstream understands liberals. The leftist hardliners know how to exploit the decency and maturity of the mainstream to manipulate us.

Let's take a look at how they do it.

3

HOW THE LEFTIST AGENDA
HAS SPREAD

We have seen how liberals, who comprise maybe 20 percent of the population, have been able to do such damage to our republic through their Long March through our cultural institutions. Dominance in those institutions allows the left to control the terms of our national discourse.

Before we look at the tactics that have given real muscle to that strategy, let's look briefly at the notion of social power. Samuel Adams tells us, "It does not take a majority to prevail . . . but rather an irate, tireless minority, keen on setting brushfires of freedom in the minds of men."

The patriots who gave us our constitutional republic understood the power of a minority determined to live in freedom. Unfortunately, the radical left understands the power of a minority determined to destroy that constitutional republic. The problem is bigger than the irate, tireless minority on the left, however, in that the mainstream majority has for too long acted like a sleeping giant when it comes to politics. And America will never be restored until mainstream Americans are as passionate about defending our culture and our Constitution as the left is about destroying them.

An awakened mainstream passion for liberty, however, will not be enough to save America. That passion has to be directed into action. Mainstream America will have to come to grips with the necessity of seizing and using political power in ways that do not naturally fit our natures. Though the tactics that we will teach in this book may seem similar at times to those of the left, the reality is that the similarity is only on the surface. The underlying foundations of liberal power and of mainstream power will be quite different.

UNDERSTANDING SOCIAL AND POLITICAL POWER

MANIPULATING THROUGH ANGER AND FEAR

It is a fact of social life that a small number of people willing to cause conflict and unpleasantness will dominate a large number of people who simply want to live in harmony. In short, "the squeaky wheel gets the grease."

We grow up seeing that the squeaky wheel does in fact get greased throughout our social lives. We have all seen families walking on eggshells to keep a difficult toddler or a thin-skinned family member from causing unpleasantness for everyone. A simple word or action that does not meet with approval from the difficult one triggers a whiny spell at best or a temper tantrum at worst.

Of course, that temper tantrum takes different forms at different ages. Sometimes the social tyrants hold their breath until they turn blue, and sometimes they bang drums in the state capitol. But the effect is the same: We learn to be careful about what we say and do around such people, and we become especially tuned in to their moods. We learn which topics are safe around them and which are off-limits.

The difficult toddler, the schoolyard bully, the thin-skinned family member, the difficult co-worker, and liberal activists all learn a simple rule: "I can get my way by threatening to make life difficult for others if I don't." They create a social electrified fence that controls where others may and may not go. They get their first taste of power through petulance.

Though they often present themselves as victims of someone else's actions, these social tyrants have a lot of power. The toddler, the thin-skinned relative, and the difficult co-worker all basically decide whether everyone around them can have a good day or a day filled with accusations, demands, and unpleasantness.

The pattern is all around us. We have all seen situations in which an irate customer in a store creates a ruckus with employees. The employees take the abuse because they have to in order to keep their jobs. Other customers don't step in for two reasons. First, it is none of our business. Mature adults learn that the world does not have to conform to our expectations. We learn to live and let live, so as we mature we develop a predisposition to stay out of things that don't directly concern us. If we don't like a particular news network, we just don't watch that network. But it wouldn't cross our minds to try to get the network banned from the airwaves so that no one else could watch it. Grown-ups mind their own business for the most part. So, we don't *condone* the behavior of the irate customer, but we leave it to the store employees and management to handle the problem.

Second, there is the deeper survival instinct in play. If we were to object aloud to the rude customer's actions, we are not sure how such a person would handle it. After all, he has already shown that he is willing to be angry, abusive, irrational, and disruptive. How far would he go? Would he become violent? Would he stalk and harass anyone who crossed him? We certainly have no evidence that he *wouldn't*.

The dynamic is the same when liberal bullies take to the streets to demand concessions from the mainstream, or when they start tossing out accusations and insults in a political discussion.

But hardcore leftists have learned throughout their lives that those who make the ruckus can make the rules, and they have found that bullying tactics work more often than not. Beneath the sweet promises of tolerance, fairness, equality, and opportunity, we find that most leftist tactics are those of the schoolyard bully.

Let's look at some of their favored tactics.

TACTIC 1: RIDE THE APPEASEMENT CYCLE
TO POWER

An especially difficult realization that we must face head-on is that those of us in the mainstream are part of the problem. We outnumber the bullies of the left by a large margin, but we have been raised to be civil and rational. Those are wonderful and helpful traits when dealing with other mainstream citizens who are also civil and rational. But they become our Achilles' heel in dealing with liberal bullies.

Out of our perfectly healthy and mature desire to live in relative harmony with others, all too often we appease the social tyrants, from the schoolyard bully to the liberal activist, in an effort to keep the peace. When liberals call us racist, we try to convince them that we are not. When they accuse us of hating the poor, we try to convince them that catastrophic debt hurts job creation, which, in turn, hurts the poor. When no amount of reasoning or evidence stops the accusations, eventually some well-meaning soul reaches across the aisle and tries to find common ground with the left in an effort to appease them.

But when we do so, we have just given our lunch money to the schoolyard bully. In the halls of Congress and on the schoolyard, the bully typically calms down just enough for us to feel that our appeasement has indeed brought us peace. But then the cycle repeats. Social bullies learn to hold out through all of our reasoning and cajoling. They learn that if they continue to whine, demand, accuse, intimidate, and threaten, we will eventually appease or compromise.

Every time the cycle repeats, the bully becomes more emboldened. Mainstream Americans learned this on the schoolyard, but we have only recently begun to realize that outfitting the bully with a protest sign or an expensive suit changes nothing. The pattern is the same.

The illustration below has brought groans of recognition from many mainstream audiences when we present it in our workshops. Most of us can see ourselves trying to reason with the unreasonable, and too often we just give in and let them win.

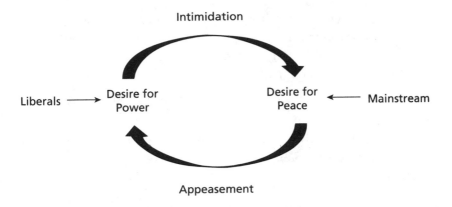

The Appeasement Cycle

THE GOLDEN RULE AND THE RUCKUS RULE

Basically, the mainstream tries to live by the Golden Rule. If we don't want others to limit our health care choices, then we don't limit the health care choices of others. If we don't want others to limit our choices of news and information, then we don't limit the choices of others. We want others to respect our desire to live our lives as we choose, within broadly agreed upon limits, and so we respect the desire of others to do the same. In so many ways, the constitutional protections of liberty can be said to derive from a deep cultural respect for the Golden Rule.

However, the left sees the maturity and responsibility of mainstream Americans as the weak point in our defenses. And, as we will see later, because the left rejects the worldview that affirms the Golden Rule, they feel no obligation to live by the standards that they set for others.

Power is the left's ambrosia, and strife is the bowl in which it is served. The left wants power. The mainstream wants peace and quiet, and the left knows that. And so we see the Appeasement Cycle played out over and over, with each cycle wearing away our liberty and increasing the power of the left. Sure enough, the left is willing to allow us peace and quiet for a time, but at a price. The price is never very high at any one time. Just compromise on this or that, conform your behavior to their demands just a tad here and there, and they'll quiet down and be nice—for a while.

The pattern of political life in the United States for the last century, complicated as it might seem on the surface, is frighteningly simple. It is the same pattern that we see with toddlers having temper tantrums to get a toy or schoolyard bullies threatening violence in order to get someone else's lunch money.

Because We Let Them

For liberal tactics to work, however, remember that the rest of us have to attempt to appease them. But appeasement didn't work when Neville Chamberlain tried it with Hitler. Instead of winning "peace in our time" by *appeasing* Hitler, he *emboldened* Hitler.

With each victory liberals achieve as a result of well-intentioned appeasement from the mainstream, they get bolder in their demands, as well as in their tactics. The parallel is striking and frightening.

In dealing with liberal bullies, the mainstream can do no better than to recall the old maxim that throwing red meat to a tiger will not turn him into a vegetarian.

We will go into more detail about the mainstream and liberal character differences behind the Appeasement Cycle in a later chapter. We will also offer tools and techniques for breaking that cycle. For now, let's just say that compromise is only sensible when both sides share the same goals. Compromise is self-destructive, however, when used to appease political bullies.

TACTIC 2: DIVIDE AND CONQUER

Identity politics is an easy way to build a power base. The stronger a group's sense of isolation and alienation from other groups, the easier it is for the left to manipulate them into voting blocs to increase their own power.

Race is an especially easy target of opportunity for spreading the leftist agenda, because it is so visible. Despite the radical left's insistence that it will take decades and cost trillions to right the wrong of past discrimination, the mainstream actually bought into Dr. King's vision fairly easily. Dr. King appealed to our heads, in that there was no rational argument in favor of treating people unfairly because of their skin color. He also appealed to our hearts, in that it just seemed wrong to treat people unfairly because of their race.

But whereas mainstreamers believe that people should be treated as individuals and that character and merit should prevail, liberals insist that rights should be parceled out based on the identity of the group. Of course, the left assures us that their intentions are pure. The surface argument—that liberals target race to make up for past discrimination—may sound credible at first. As is the case with most liberal claims, however, this argument does not hold up under close scrutiny.

How do liberals explain their savaging of Justice Clarence Thomas or black conservatives supported by the Tea Party? Instead of supporting black conservatives "to make up for past discrimination," we hear the stupefying claim that they are "not black enough."[27] For the left, "black" seems to be more of a voting bloc than a race.

How do liberals explain the damage done to poor families, and most notably to poor black families, as a result of decades of liberal policies?[28] Nothing short of catastrophic, those results cannot be explained away as unintended consequences of good intentions, since the liberal policies and their effects have been evident for decades. One would have to try *not* to see the social havoc wrought when welfare bureaucrats usurp the father's role in the family.

So if liberals cannot claim to be ignorant of the damage caused by their policies, we can only conclude that the results are acceptable to them, if not intentional. After all, who benefits from the creation of a permanent underclass, a disproportionate percentage of whom are black and most of whom feel alienated from the rest of society? White liberals benefit at every election from a massive black vote, they own the votes of the poor, and they have no incentive to correct their course in order to promote real prosperity.

Studies show beyond doubt that children of married couples are far less likely to live in poverty than those born out of wedlock.[29] Out-of-wedlock births, however, have skyrocketed, particularly in black communities, since liberals began their social experimentation in the 1960s. But anyone who questions the wisdom of subsidizing out-of-wedlock births is accused of hating the poor or being racist.

The left's opposition to border security and their opposition to all efforts to assimilate immigrants seem designed to grow yet another bloc of alienated and resentful voters. Having progressively alienated more and more voters, the left desperately needs to import, polarize, and register new voters, dead or alive, legal or illegal. A popular threat among left-wing radicals in the 1960s was that they would impose their will upon the rest of us "by any means necessary." And they are making good on that threat.

Women against men, old against young, race against race, on and on the liberal scythe separates and polarizes people who would otherwise be united by bonds of family, neighborhood, community, tradition, and country.

As always, ask yourself one question: Who benefits from all the divisiveness? The answer will always be the same: liberal politicians.

TACTIC 3: PLAY THE VICTIM GAME

Related to the tactic of polarizing groups is the even more sinister method of singling out some groups to be villains in the political drama and casting others as helpless victims. Leftists reassure the selected victim group that the villains have oppressed them and must be made to pay. In so doing, the left plays to the basest and meanest side of humanity, the side that envies the accomplishments of others, the side that wants revenge or an easy way out.

And of course the left positions themselves as the heroes in the drama. They will make everything right for the victim and punish the villain. All the liberals need in return is for the victims to vote for the liberal heroes, to give them power and resources, and, above all, not to question their authority, or, apparently, their results.

And no bounds of logic or reason can interfere with the left when playing the Victim Game. A black female banker who starts her own business can easily fall into multiple categories. As a black female, she is the victim of white males. As a banker and entrepreneur, she is a villain who oppresses poor people and employees of her business. Bankers are painted as villains by the left when they engage in sound lending practices and as victims deserving a bailout when they make bad loans.

On the surface, trying to follow liberal logic is as exhausting as trying to follow Bill Clinton at a beauty pageant. There are so many sudden pivots and switchbacks. But beneath the surface contradictions, we find a common factor: All liberal positions are designed to increase the power of liberals over the rest of us. As long as the votes and contributions roll in, neither consistency nor consequences seem to matter to the hardcore left.

Besides, liberals have another tactic that absolves them of any responsibility for inconsistency or hypocrisy.

TACTIC 4: WORDS MEAN WHAT LIBERALS WANT THEM TO MEAN

Mainstreamers are often struck by the inconsistency between the way liberals use words and what those words actually mean. For example, we have already mentioned "racist" as one of the most commonly used words in liberal speech. What is stunning about the liberal use of the word, however, is that it actually has nothing to do with racism.

RACISTS, SEXISTS, AND HATERS! OH MY!

If you are opposed to preferential treatment based on race (e.g., affirmative action), you are branded a racist. If a liberal black politician makes an absurd statement and you point out the absurdity of the statement, you are called a racist. On the other hand, if you argue for preferential treatment or tolerate absurdity because the speaker is a black liberal, then, according to liberals, you're an enlightened champion for racial equality.

Even more bizarre in the left's use of the word "racist" is that the issue in question usually doesn't even have to do with race in any way. Jimmy Carter's trained nose sniffed out the fumes of racism in the mainstream's opposition to Obamacare.[30] That's it! If you don't want some Washington bureaucrat making decisions about your family's health care, you must be a racist!

Liberals routinely describe as "sexist" anyone who thinks that men and women differ in their predispositions to math and science skills.[31] At Harvard, Larry Summers mentioned differences in mathematical achievement between males and females, and female professors demanded his head on a platter. So much for being tolerant of people with diverse views.

And never mind the fact that women outperform men on measures of verbal achievement! It's hard to convince people they have been victims of oppression if you mention that they outperform the group that is supposedly oppressing them. "Sexist" means what liberals want it to mean.

The mainstream would reserve the use of the term "sexist" for anyone who believes that women are *inferior* to men—you know, like having to cover their faces in public. But leftists attacked as sexist anyone who resisted Hillary Clinton's attempt to take over our health care system. (Hang in there if you remembered that opposition to socialized medicine is supposed to be *racist*.) And mentioning Hillary's pantsuits in an unflattering manner was proof positive of chauvinistic, sexist barbarity. Yet the left was not only tolerant of people who attacked Sarah Palin's intelligence, or even those who made her wardrobe a campaign issue in 2008, the left was actually leading the attack.

The inconsistency disappears, obviously, when we realize that liberals don't use words to communicate ideas and convey information the way the rest of us do. Liberals use words as either carrots or sticks, that is, as ways of manipulating others. Words have only one purpose for liberals, and that is increasing their power and control.

Calling names to create a diversion is an age-old leftist tactic. Pat Buchanan has pointed out that communists back in the 1930s were advising their followers to describe opponents as "fascist, or Nazi, or anti-Semitic" in order to silence them.[32] As we will see when we discuss worldviews in more depth, it's not coincidence that Joseph Goebbels advised fellow Nazis that if they told a lie often enough, people would start to believe it. As we will see, when it comes to a fundamental worldview, the communists and Nazis had more in common than they would admit. The truly frightening thing is how much they both have in common with the foundational beliefs of American liberalism.

Words like "tolerance," "diversity," "hope," and "change" are carrot words for liberals. As long as we don't delve too deeply into what the left actually *does* when they use those words, they sound pretty good. Who could have a problem with tolerance? Who could oppose diversity?

Well, liberals can and do, if by "tolerance" you mean allowing people to listen to radio commentators that liberals don't like, or if by "diversity" you mean that people might differ in skills and abilities, or might want to choose from diverse health care options. For the left, the purpose of those pleasant-sounding words is not to convey a concept that can be applied logically across a range of situations; it is merely to lure the uninformed and misinformed into the political orbit of the liberal. To liberals, certain words seem to have no consistent, objective meaning in and of themselves.

The same rule applies for liberal "stick" words. "Racist," "sexist," "hatemonger," and "greedy" have no inherent and consistent meaning for liberals that would enable a reasonable listener to discern and apply a set of standards in order to evaluate an accusation. Leftists do not use words to communicate meaning; they use words for impact. And the impact they want is to control others by putting them on the defensive. The seeming inconsistencies and contradictions described above become perfectly consistent when viewed in this light. In fact, they *only* make sense when viewed in this light.

- "Racist" is liberal for "You're not making me happy and I hate you."
- "Sexist" is liberal for "You're not making me happy and I hate you."
- "Hatemonger" is liberal for "You're not making me happy and I hate you."
- "Greedy" is liberal for "You're not making me happy and I hate you."

Of course, liberals are not *that* simplistic. There have to be variations and fine-tuning to fit various circumstances. For example:

- "McCarthyism" is liberal for "You've found me out and I hate you."
- "Intolerant" is liberal for "You don't share my views and I hate you."
- "Unfair" is liberal for "I don't like the outcome and I hate you."
- "Stupid" is liberal for "I don't understand and I hate you."

Note that the seeming hypocrisy of liberal speech vanishes if we understand what liberals are really saying. If they want the government to seize health care and you don't, then any of the stick words simply mean that you're not making them happy and they hate you. The actual meaning of words doesn't matter to liberals; only the effect matters.

FIRST-AMENDMENT FOLLIES

Let's look at the bizarre ways liberals use the words of the First Amendment. Think back to the scandal a few years ago when an artist received public money for dropping a crucifix in a jar of urine and calling it a creative work of art. People in the mainstream were understandably outraged, both at the insult to the religious beliefs of millions of Americans and also at the flagrant waste of taxpayers' money.[33]

The left's response to our concerns was outrage! We were engaging in *censorship*, they claimed. Challenging the tax-paid immersion of a crucifix in a jar of urine was tantamount to *establishing a state religion*! Could the Inquisition be far behind, with creative geniuses broken on the rack by right-wing philistines? And state-funded radio supported the noble artistes beleaguered by backward taxpayers by playing musical classics that had once been censored by European monarchs.

Nudge, nudge. Get it? If you don't want your tax dollars subsidizing some artiste to urinate in a jar, you are just a step away from burning books and torturing heretics. We heard mind-numbing lectures from the left on the importance of tolerance and the evils of censorship. The battle cry of the open-mindedness brigade was the stupefying "Who are we to judge what is and what is not a work of art?"

It's easy to imagine a conversation between two liberals lauding a jar of urine with a crucifix in it as if it were the *Mona Lisa*, all the while sounding quite sophisticated:

> "*I find it oddly provocative, in a whimsical, irreverent kind of way. What do you think, Ché?*"
>
> "*Oh, I'm captivated by the subtle interplay of light and shadow, as if the artist is challenging each of us to search out the light and shadow within us.*"
>
> "*And such a better use of tax money than buying bombers for the Air Force!*"
>
> "*Oh, most decidedly so! More Chablis?*"

The silliness of the left's arguments in cases like this almost disguises the danger of what they're up to. Fast-forward to recent memory, when all around the country leftists have challenged any display of the Ten Commandments in public buildings or any other acknowledgments of our Judeo-Christian roots.[34] Once again, they drag out the First

Amendment and pretend to be concerned that the display of such a thing establishes a state church. Here comes the Inquisition again!

But note the dizzying inconsistency. If liberals insist that a crucifix in a jar of urine is an artistic masterpiece protected by the First Amendment, could we not say that a granite carving of the Ten Commandments in a county courthouse is also a work of art protected by that same standard? After all, using their own commonly professed standards, who are we to judge what is and what is not a work of art? If a crucifix in a jar of urine qualifies as a work of art for the left, the artistic bar would seem to be set fairly low. Surely a carving in granite of a historic code might be able to squeak past such a standard.

If, as the left loves to tell us, the purpose of art is to challenge us, why then should only the mainstream be challenged?[35] Why is it not permissible for the left to be challenged by the Ten Commandments when they enter a public building?

The crucifix in urine and the Ten Commandments in a county courthouse are both artistic representations of objects that have religious, cultural, and historical significance. Both were paid for with taxpayers' money. The only difference in the two cases is that one has been dipped in urine.

So what is the rule of law that applies here from the liberal point of view?

- Religious symbol dipped in urine: *protected by the First Amendment.*
- Religious symbol not dipped in urine: *forbidden by the First Amendment.*

Rational human beings might reasonably seek some consistency in application of the First Amendment to works of art funded with taxpayers' money by asking questions such as

- If the definition of art is subjective, why can't we consider granite carvings of the Ten Commandments to be works of art and therefore protected rather than prohibited by the First Amendment?

- Why is a religious symbol dipped in urine protected by the First Amendment and one not dipped in urine forbidden by that same amendment?
- If carvings of the Ten Commandments were dipped in urine, then could they be displayed on public property?
- Does it have to be real urine, or could we substitute something else like, say, lemon juice?
- Is immersion necessary, or would sprinkling suffice?
- Why could we not consider a public prayer to be a form of "performance art" protected by the First Amendment?

Absurd though the above might seem at first glance, even the most fleeting attempt at intellectual consistency by the left would demand that they either accept public display of the Ten Commandments as artwork protected by the First Amendment or that they answer the questions about the mystical powers of urine.

And that is, of course, the point: Liberals make no attempt at intellectual consistency, even of the fleeting variety, in the positions they take. They don't use words in the same manner that the rest of us do.

The consistency is there, just at a deeper level. "Whimsical and provocative art protected by the First Amendment" simply means to liberals: "I'm dipping something valuable to you in urine, I'm debasing it and insulting you, and, on top of that, I'm making you pay for it! And you can't stop me!"

"You're imposing your religion on me" just means to liberals: "I don't like what I see and I can make you take it down."

Either way, liberals experience the exhilaration of power over others so familiar to the schoolyard bully, and the mainstream falls for the idea that we are powerless to do anything about it. Later we will talk about the importance of recognizing the unspoken narrative in exchanges with the left. For now, just listen for the faint tones of the classic schoolyard taunt: "I can do this to you and you can't stop me! *NAH-nah-nah-NAH-nah!*"

On the playground, children stick out their tongues for emphasis. In the courthouse, liberals call the ACLU.

One of the worst things that mainstream candidates and activists can do is to get suckered into responding to liberal attack words. Clarification and explanations are pointless. Liberals don't misunderstand the meaning of the words they use. They don't misunderstand the First Amendment or the Constitution. They just don't care about any of that. They only care about getting their way and having power over others.

TACTIC 5: DON'T DEBATE, ATTACK

The liberal playbook should be coming into clearer relief now. Raise a ruckus and peace-loving people will appease you. Polarize and divide people. Play the Victim Game. Use words as sticks and carrots to manipulate others.

Each of these are important in their own right, but they all come together in the cardinal tactic of liberal politics. Liberals don't explain themselves. They don't debate. They don't account for discrepancies between what they profess and what they actually do.

Liberals always attack.

If liberals were confronted with the above logic about the First Amendment, they wouldn't try to defend the crucifix in urine as a work of art or explain why a carving of the Ten Commandments isn't a work of art. They would call the questioner a "religious nut" and change the subject.

If you questioned them about why Hillary Clinton represents women's interests but Sarah Palin doesn't, they would just say that you don't understand women's issues. Or they would call you a tea bagger. The actual content of the attack isn't as important to them as being *on* the attack. Leftists could give eels lessons on the art of being slippery.

The mainstream has never figured out how to counter this tactic. Over and over we see mainstream citizens and politicians falling for liberal attacks and ending up on the defensive. Obama seizes the health care system of three hundred million people against our will, and we end up explaining that we *do* want poor children to have medical care. We timidly raise questions about liberal teachers using their position to indoctrinate children, and we end up explaining that we have nothing against teachers.

No matter how absurd, inconsistent, or hypocritical the charge made by liberals, the mainstream tries to use logic and facts to prove our innocence.

The mainstream fails to see that we have already lost the battle the instant we go on the defensive. Isolating and attacking the target is right out of *Rules for Radicals* by Saul Alinsky, the playbook for radical left-wing "community organizers" like Barack Obama.[36] Anyone who stands in the way of the radical left's agenda is attacked and demonized. Doctors, insurance companies, drug companies, auto executives, news networks that aren't in their pocket, radio commentators they don't like, taxpayers who attend Tea Party protests—all of these have had their turn as demon-of-the-day.

Logic and facts have never convinced hardcore liberals, and they never will. And allowing liberals to put us on the defensive and keep us there only emboldens them. Eventually we have to learn that trying to explain mainstream thinking to hardcore leftists is like trying to teach a rattlesnake to do the fox-trot—the dancing will be ugly and you will get bitten to boot.

TACTIC 6: HIDE THE TRUE AGENDA

By now it should be obvious that liberals can't talk about their true intention—to try to force the rest of us into a mold designed by liberals—without being laughed at, trounced at the polls, and ridden out of town on a rail. Can you imagine a campaign platform that says, "We know better than you do how you should live your life, so we're going to take your resources and make your decisions for you?" The only funding source they'd have left would be George Soros.

There couldn't be a better example of hiding true liberal intentions than the global warming scam.[37] For a few million years now, the planet's climate has cycled between warming and cooling periods. If you are fortunate enough to live during one of the warming trends, you have abundant water and excellent growing conditions for food. And, as a bonus, the warmer climate allows you to grow grapes for wine farther north, as the Europeans found during the Medieval Warm Period. If you draw the short straw and live during a cooling period, on the other hand, you face droughts and famine—the water that could support crops is tied up in the polar ice caps and a plague of glaciers.[38]

So liberals take something like a climate that's going to change regardless of what we do, come up with a theory to say not only that it's bad but also that it's our fault, and then conclude that we need higher taxes and more government.

If liberals were really concerned about greenhouse gasses, wouldn't they have something to say about Al Gore flying all over the world in his private jet, belching greenhouse gasses into the air? And that private jet probably belches lots of greenhouse gasses in its own right.

Predictably, not a single liberal proposal to save the earth, improve the best health care system on the planet, educate children, save our economy, or light a dark room has ever advocated lower taxes and less government as the key. Lower taxes and less government deprive the left of their need for power and control.

TACTIC 7: CONTROL THROUGH CONFUSION

All the previous tactics cast the left in the clearly dominant role in some way. But there are situations, such as the debt-ceiling debate after the 2010 election, in which the left has taken a good old country butt-whipping from the electorate, and they are in a desperate struggle to regain the upper hand.

In such cases, the left pulls out one of their most bizarre tactics, calling in fire on their own position in order to create confusion in the minds of the uninformed and misinformed voters. Strange as it may seem on the surface, the confusion actually buys the left time to regain control of the political battlefield.

It's this tactic that prevents the mainstream majority from correcting the nation's course after landslide victories, so it's critical for the mainstream to understand and learn to counter it.

The tactic is actually quite simple. When the left is on the defensive and the mainstream has gained ground, the left changes the narrative to blame *both sides* for the nation's woes. In the new narrative, the solution is not that the left has taken a beating, but instead that both sides need to work together.

When they have been overrun by the mainstream on an issue, such as the ruinous debt that resulted in the Republican landslide of 2010, the first step is to counterattack to break the mainstream's advance. In 2011 they did this with the infamous ads about the new Congress trying to push Granny over a cliff. The idea here is to distract attention from the reasons that turned the tide of battle against them to begin with—in this case, Obamacare, bailouts, pork bills, an economy sunk by liberal policies, and trillions in new debt. Of course, part of the counterattack is to threaten to shut down the government and then blame it on the newcomers.

The next step is the tricky one: changing the political narrative so that *both* the mainstream *and* the left appear to be taking fire. Liberal institutions begin to call for "both sides" to calm down and "work together" to solve the crisis. The left's institutions seem to be firing on their own soldiers as well as the recently elected mainstreamers. But remember that the left was *already* under fire from the voters who threw them out in the last election—the left was already on the defensive—so they actually lose nothing when they employ this tactic. But the gain for the left is that the mainstream now comes under fire as well, and the momentum of the mainstream is broken.

Uninformed and misinformed voters lose sight of the original issues in the fog created by the narrative that "both sides" share blame for the crisis. Voters who are not seasoned political activists, those who do not recognize the left's diversionary tactic, begin to hear in the news media that a crisis is looming—such as a government "shutdown" or default on the debt—and they grow tired of the fighting. After all, the rest of us are not political animals, and we do not have the stomach for a prolonged fight. The known devil—ruinous debt and corrupt spending—is better than the chaos, confusion, and uncertainty being trumpeted in the media's narrative.

Of course, the media's narrative about the need for "working together" begins to take hold among the uninformed and misinformed, and, sure enough, the media begins to produce polls claiming that voters are fed up with the political fighting and just want a solution to the "crisis."

And the solution, of course, is to run through the Appeasement Cycle again. So, after trouncing the left at the polls, mainstream politicians are now surrounded by advice to "reach across the aisle" and to "work together to get things done."

The left's media dominance has allowed them to change the narrative from "the people are fed up with the left and the tide has turned against them" to "both sides need to stop the craziness and work together." And when the mainstream "works together" with the radical left, government grows and liberty shrinks.

Once the "work together" theme is in play in the minds of the uninformed and misinformed, the left has won. Even though the left in this narrative paints their own side as sharing some guilt with the mainstream for the chaos, the left's goal all along has been to break the mainstream's advance, and they have done it. The left has lost nothing. Their advance may have slowed down a bit, but that's all.

How do we defeat this insidious tactic? Uninformed and misinformed voters are the key. As we will see, the first step will be for mainstream politicians to stop surrendering control of the narrative to the left in the first place, as we always do. To do this, we need mainstream citizens outside of formal politics serving as political militia, controlling the narrative around dinner tables, by the coffee machine at the office, in line at the grocery store, and anywhere people talk about what's going on.

And the Tea Party needs to turn out demonstrations after the elections that are as big as those before the elections in order to keep the focus where it belongs: on the ruinous problems brought about by liberal policies. That will counteract the left's disinformation campaign coming from their fifth column in the media. The third step is to eventually break the left's hold on the media so that the public gets information instead of leftist propaganda in the first place.

We will cover methods for doing that in later chapters.

WHAT THEN MUST WE DO?

The first step in changing our tactics is to understand why our tactics haven't worked. To understand that, we need to better understand not just what liberals do, their strategies and tactics, but *why they do it*. We have to understand the worldview and the mentality that would drive someone to crave power over others, a worldview that would condone false accusations as a normal course of doing business, that would promote division and suspicion instead of a sense of belonging to a greater whole, that hides its true agenda under a façade of happy talk, that drops a crucifix in a jar of urine and calls it protected speech while banning the Ten Commandments from public buildings.

We have to explore the cold, dark origins of the leftist worldview.

4

WE LIVE IN TWO
DIFFERENT WORLDS

"We hold these truths to be self-evident, that all men are created equal, that they are endowed by their Creator with certain unalienable Rights, that among these are Life, Liberty and the pursuit of Happiness—That to secure these rights, Governments are instituted among Men, deriving their just powers from the consent of the governed . . ."
—Declaration of Independence

"When you spread the wealth around, it's good for everyone."
—Barack Obama to Joe the Plumber in 2008 Presidential Campaign

THROUGH A GLASS DARKLY

Throughout history, humans have looked in the sky at night and seen billions of stars. We know now that there are billions of galaxies, each with billions of stars. Everywhere we look we see that nature is orderly, and that the very existence of human consciousness depends upon physical factors that are stunningly complex.

It is in our nature to wonder at such things, to ask how they came to be and how we came to be, and to ask what we are to make of what we see. It is our nature to wonder where we fit in this world. And though science has given us many answers to many questions, while we are in this world, as Saint Paul told us, "we look through a glass darkly." There are some fundamental questions that just cannot be answered by science. At some point, we view the evidence around us, including the scientific evidence of physics, cosmology, probability, information theory, and biology, and then we draw conclusions that are acts of faith.

The nature of that faith is where the mainstream and liberal world-views part company.

So let us look at our second question: How are liberals different from the mainstream?

QUESTIONS OF FAITH

From Darwinism to global warming, the left loves to tell us that science is superior to faith. No one in the mainstream would question that the scientific method can help us to understand the world and the people in it up to a point, or that the scientific method has brought us a long way in understanding *how* the world works, or that it has dramatically improved our quality of life. But there are always questions that cannot be answered by science. Besides, science can give us knowledge, but it cannot give us wisdom.

Why is there something rather than nothing in the universe? Was the universe created, or did it just belch into existence on its own? And what about us? Is human life the result of an intelligent Creator, or did life just evolve through blind chemical processes with no purpose, no guidance, and no meaning to our existence other than that which we give it?

Asking those questions is anything but an idle academic pastime. Our answers to those questions shape our worldview, our beliefs about the world, about why things are the way they are, and about how we should behave in the world. If the universe was created, then whoever or whatever created it might have some claim on us, some standards that we need to seek and follow. On the other hand, if the universe just belched forth one day on its own, then our existence is as meaningless as that of the universe itself, and there can be no moral reference point other than the standards that we set for ourselves, and those are completely arbitrary.

What do these questions have to do with mainstream versus liberal politics? Everything. Because *everyone* has some kind of faith, everyone makes some fundamental nonscientific assumptions about how things came to be and what it all means.

One set of faith assumptions, those on which America was founded, holds that we are "endowed by our Creator with certain unalienable rights." That faith leads to limited government and respect for the rights of individuals. Those are the assumptions shared by mainstream Americans, including, oddly enough, many of the uninformed and misinformed voters who frequently vote with the left.

The other faith is the one on which Marxism rests, and it leads to a dog-eat-dog quest for power in which no tactic is out of bounds. That worldview leads to politicians who believe that they have the right to take the earnings of some and spread them around to others, especially if those others return the favor with political contributions.

American liberalism is a direct descendant of this latter faith. As Ezekiel says, "As is the mother, so is her daughter."[39]

Though much has been written about the finer points of various worldviews[40] and about worldviews in the political realm,[41] our intentions here are purely practical and not academic. We want mainstream activists and candidates to be able to quickly recognize and expose the worldview that lurks underneath so much of the sweet rhetoric of liberalism. Consequently, we want to keep our method simple so that it can be used in the heat of debate, and we will focus only on those elements of worldviews that separate the mainstream from the left.

ROOTS OF THE CURRENT CONFLICT

It is generally accepted that the Judeo-Christian worldview that shaped America was passed down from Judaism and Christianity in the Middle East, through the Greco-Roman world and their philosophers, then through the European world of the Middle Ages, and finally to us in the mainstream of American life.[42] Anyone who has taken high school geometry knows the importance that the early Greeks placed on objective truth. It wasn't enough to say that one line *looked* longer than another; the statement had to be proven.

This idea of objectively verifiable truth continued through the ages with philosophers like Saint Thomas Aquinas, who presented proofs for the existence of God that were based on these logical methods handed down from the ancient Greeks. For example, Aquinas argued, following Aristotle, that all things have a cause, and if we track those back in time, there must have been something that started the whole process. Thus the need for a "first cause," something outside of nature that got nature started, was one early proof of the existence of God.[43]

Though we might quibble here and there about specifics, some of the aspects of the Judeo-Christian worldview are these:

- The universe did not just happen on its own; God exists.
- The material, physical reality is not the only reality.
- God created human beings through some kind of intentional action or process; we are not the accidental result of purely random processes.
- Because God created human beings—through whatever process—human beings are important and our lives have meaning and purpose.
- Good and evil, truth and falsehood exist; they are not just social inventions.
- Human beings have the capacity to choose our actions, and we are responsible for those choices.

In essence, these are the faith assumptions of the mainstream worldview. Their origins may be in Judaism and Christianity as religions, but these assumptions are now woven into the values, habits, and language of mainstream American culture. So someone who has never darkened the door of a church or synagogue could say that Obama has no "right" to take our earnings and give them to his voters and contributors. Such an objection appeals to a standard of right and wrong that is higher than the speaker's preferences or Obama's preferences, a standard that is woven into our culture, regardless that standard's origins in formal religion.

As philosophers wrestled with difficult questions, such as how to resolve the goodness of God with the suffering and misery clearly evident in the world, or how to resolve the power of God with the freedom of human beings to act, variations on these basic Judeo-Christian themes emerged.

Alongside these philosophical developments, science began to be more of a hands-on activity than just philosophical speculation. Galileo, Kepler, Newton, and others began to chart nature, the physical aspect of reality, with increasing precision. God's creation was placed under the microscope and probed with telescopes; it was described using the languages of mathematics and science. In fact, to many of history's most brilliant scientists, the beauty and perfection of mathematics itself pointed to a Creator.

The rational approach of early scientists was consistent with the Judeo-Christian worldview: A rational Being created an orderly world, and rational study by His creatures simply revealed the beauty and majesty of that divinely ordered world. Religion and science were not enemies.

With René Descartes, the distinction between the spiritual world and the material world came into sharper focus. He argued that the material world, including human beings, functioned mechanically, as a result of physical cause-and-effect processes. Our bodies were amazing machines, but they were machines nonetheless. Our souls interacted with our material bodies, but our material bodies functioned just like those of any animal.[44] God may have created the material world, but it ran on its own. Still, through the soul interacting with the material body, we could experience and understand the world around us.

CROSSING THE NATURALIST BRIDGE

In an emerging theme among many philosophers and scientists, the balance between the spiritual and material worlds tipped more and more toward the material. The physical world seemed to function in an orderly manner in its own right; it seemed to be self-sufficient. In Deist thinking, God was no longer necessary as the personal, rational Being with Whom human beings had a connection and Who sustained the physical world. God simply became the Creator, the one Who made the machine and set it in motion, but nothing else. That view enabled some to maintain belief in God while recognizing that nature seemed to run on its own like a well-oiled machine.[45]

For still others, God became an abstraction, the sum of all natural laws. For Hegel, God wasn't so much a Being Who exists independently of the world but was instead a Spirit or Thought that was evolving, and the Judeo-Christian worldview was just one passing step in that evolution.

One of Hegel's followers, Ludwig Feuerbach, took this rejection of the Judeo-Christian worldview even further. For Feuerbach, God was simply a projection of the ideals of humanity. In a sense, he argued, man created God in our minds. Nature, however, the material world, was real, and that was the starting point for everything else. Religion would not make us better; only improvement in our material conditions would.[46]

If you think this is starting to sound like the "social justice" being preached from leftist pulpits, then you see where we're heading. ⚡

It was out of this path that the worldview known as "naturalism" or "materialism" developed, the belief that everything is matter and that nothing else exists, that the physical world and the laws of physics are all there is.

And here is the crucial break with the Judeo-Christian worldview. If the physical world is all there is, then it follows that our moral sense is also the result of physical processes and nothing more. Because there can be no objective, external source of morality, humans are then free to develop whatever moral code suits them.

The stream of thought that had its source in the Judeo-Christian worldview had reached a fork. The Judeo-Christian stream continued to flow, but now there was another stream that diverged more and more from its source. Both streams have collided in today's America, and the political turbulence that we see around us has as its source these conflicting worldviews.

So, with humans looking more and more like the rest of nature, just matter in motion, even the way in which we know what we know came under scrutiny. Our capacity to directly perceive reality in a rational and objective way (as rational beings created by a rational Being) gave ground to a view emphasizing the chemical and nervous processes by which we perceive the world. It seemed apparent that at least some aspects of reality belonged in a different and more subjective category.

For example, how could we prove that *red* looks the same to us as it does to someone else? The light itself was objective, real; it could be measured in wavelengths. Our perception of the color of that light, however, was private, subjective. But the world was still *real*, even if we viewed it through subjective filters.

PHILOSOPHY HITS BOTTOM: THE NIHILIST WORLDVIEW

More skeptical philosophers, however, pushed this idea of the subjective nature of perception to its logical extreme. How do we know that the wavelength of light that we measure in the laboratory is any more real, any more objective, than our private experience of redness? After all, we "saw" ourselves measuring the wavelength, but the act of *seeing* happened inside of our own minds.

Skepticism, so healthy and useful in moderation, had reached its extreme conclusion. How do we know that the tree or the person we are looking at exists anywhere but inside of our minds? Ultimately, the whole of our experience happens inside our heads and is therefore wholly subjective. How can we truly *know* anything outside of our heads? In fact, a question that occupied these philosophers (and many a college sophomore) was: How do we even know that we really exist at all?

To these skeptics, the distinction between objective reality and subjective perception became a false one; private or subjective experience is all that we can know. According to this view, everything that we experience is ultimately subjective, inside the mind of each of us as individuals, and it is not possible to truly know anything outside of our own subjective experience. The idea of objective reality, the idea of truth outside of us, was hopelessly lost. Our world and our truth are *constructed* in our own minds. They do not exist in reality. We can't be sure of anything.

And with the Divine out of the picture, we were on our own.

Taken to the logical conclusion, this worldview is described as "nihilism," the belief that there is no real truth and no meaning. Nothing is any better or truer than anything else; nothing can be known accurately or objectively. There is no right and wrong, only what is.

"God is dead," Nietzsche told us as he followed Feuerbach's path of naturalism to nihilism, its logical conclusion. There could be no fixed reference point for morality. There could be no "good" and no "evil" in a world in which everything is permitted. Nothing is true. Nothing is better than anything else. Nietzsche even imagined that human beings would eventually evolve who would transcend our primitive beliefs in right and wrong and who would have the "will to power." This new race would be the Supermen, strong, powerful, and setting their own standards of right and wrong.[47]

Some naturalists have tried stay off the path to nihilism by constructing ethics that are somehow consistent with a naturalist worldview. They argue that human consciousness may be merely the accidental result of physical processes, but once we have that consciousness, we can make moral choices. Or they argue that humans evolved a sense of morality because morality had survival value for the species. Thus humans evolved a tendency to share because those who shared were given more mating choices, so their genes made it into the gene pool. Sharing isn't good for any reason other than its supposed contribution to the survival of the species.

But these arguments easily fall apart. On what basis would we make moral choices if nothing exists but atoms and molecules moving according to physical laws? Atoms and molecules following the laws of physics could never be wrong; they could only do what they do. So couldn't greed also be said to have survival value? If I hoard all my resources, I can survive and find lots of mates, and my genes make it into the gene pool. And besides, why is survival actually any better than extinction? Both are just natural processes. We may *like* one better than the other, but we cannot assign a moral value to either.

Like it or not, fully fledged naturalism leads inevitably to fully fledged nihilism. If there is no Creator, if human life is a purely accidental result of blind physical processes, there can be no right or wrong, only things that we personally like and things that we personally dislike.

The naturalist or materialist worldview, and its nihilist implications, can be summarized as follows:

- The universe has either always existed or it came into existence on its own; there is no Creator.
- All life, including human life, evolved purely by chance through blind physical processes.
- Human beings have no special significance in the universe, and we cannot turn to anything or anyone outside of that physical system.
- There can be no objectively real standards of truth, beauty, or right and wrong; a jar of urine holding a crucifix has as much claim to being a work of art as does the *Mona Lisa*.

- All morals are simply social habits, customs that developed because they served some survival value for some members of society. Right and wrong are subjective, and there is no external standard by which to tell one from the other.

FROM WORLDVIEWS TO POLITICS

In the broadest terms, much of the struggle in American politics today is between the descendants of these two worldviews. One follows the Judeo-Christian path and holds, essentially, that right and wrong exist, that human beings are special in all of nature, that we can discern truth from falsehood, and that we are responsible for our own actions. This worldview, espoused by our Founding Fathers, underlies the belief that liberty is the natural state of human beings. And it was that worldview that shaped American culture and the character of our people.

The other worldview follows the naturalist and nihilist path and holds that right and wrong are subjective, private experiences that have no external basis in reality. There are no standards of right and wrong, and there are no absolutes. The universe follows the natural laws of physics, and we are nothing more than part of the universe. Humans are nothing special, just chemical processes that came together in a certain way and that do certain things. We might have ethical values, but those are just the result of our heredity and environmental conditioning and are no better or worse than any other ethical values. They just are.

This worldview is the philosophical basis of Nazism and communism.[48] If we follow this latter train of thought to American liberalism in the twenty-first century, we find people who defend Darwinism with missionary zeal, people who insist that our morality can be reduced to personal preferences and social habits, and people who denigrate the fundamental beliefs of the Judeo-Christian worldview. And when we follow the implications of that worldview, they lead inevitably to the cold, dark heart of leftist philosophy.

With this background, let's take our worldviews down to the voting booth. Let's look at the political implications of the mainstream and liberal worldviews.

Shaped by our Judeo-Christian worldview, the mainstream is likely to have political beliefs that

- Our rights come from our Creator and not from government.
- Human beings are capable of good and evil; we make choices and, barring some obvious disability, we are responsible for our actions and for the consequences of those actions, both good and bad.
- Because some statements are true and some are false, we can use evidence and reason to find out which are which.
- As morally responsible beings, our natural state is liberty; only in a free society can human beings choose their actions and reap the consequences of those choices.
- People who make good choices should enjoy the fruits of those choices; people who make bad choices should face the consequences of those choices. In fact, the consequences of bad choices provide a form of moral education.
- Some standards seem right even if they are inconvenient for us; they stand on their own regardless of any advantage or disadvantage that they might give us. These would include, for instance, that we should work for what we get, that we should not steal the property of others, that we should not lie, that we should not murder, and that we should voluntarily help those who cannot help themselves.
- Parents should support their children and teach them to be responsible for themselves and to respect the rights of others.

Notice that the mainstream worldview fits well with the notion of individual liberty that is limited only in ways that have widespread mutual benefits. We can only live as responsible, moral beings if we live in a state of liberty. We are responsible to use our talents to take care of ourselves and our families, and we should voluntarily share with those who cannot help themselves. Taking what people have earned for purposes other than widely shared purposes and benefits (e.g., military defense, public roads, fire and police protection, protecting our borders) is tantamount to stealing. Because human beings have a dark side and are capable of great evil, they cannot be trusted with power over others. Power must therefore be dispersed, and the barriers to using it must be high to prevent a small number of people from imposing their will on the rest.

Now look at the political implications of the leftist worldview. In essence, dogmatic liberalism is based on assumptions and beliefs that have variously been called naturalistic, materialistic, humanistic, or nihilistic. Though the specifics of these worldviews differ, they all are based in a rejection of the Judeo-Christian worldview and its fixed point of reference for morality. The political implications of the leftist worldview are as follows

- Because the universe exists on its own, and there are no moral standards outside of those we set for ourselves, our form of government will be based on human ends and not guided by any principles from a Creator.
- Rights are socially constructed ideas; they have no significance of their own and no source other than social custom; and, because rights are socially constructed ideas, they have been defined by those in power to benefit those in power.
- Because rights are arbitrary social conventions, they can be redefined as one group taking power from another; for example, there is nothing to stop a group in power from discovering a right "not to be offended" by political views with which they disagree.

These are the implications that follow most obviously and easily from the materialist worldview, and they are the ones that come to the surface most clearly in the writings of the cultural Marxists. Now it becomes clear why traditional religion was one of the three most important cultural targets for radical leftists. Traditional religion was not only a problem in itself; it tended to influence the culture and, through the culture, the character of people who did not subscribe to formal religious beliefs.

When Barack Obama criticized our Constitution because it granted "negative rights" that limited government instead of "positive rights" by which we could demand certain benefits from government, he was being fully consistent with this idea that rights can come and go based on human will. With no Creator setting an outside standard for government actions or for the rights of people, we have a lot of room in which to define how we want things to be.

IF YOU SAY A, YOU MUST SAY B

But there are other implications of the materialist worldview, the view that we are here only because of blind evolutionary processes with no absolute standards of morality. These follow logically from the materialist worldview, and they influence liberal policies, but hardcore liberals want to keep these implications far from public awareness. Uninformed and misinformed liberal voters would be repulsed by these implications if they ever became aware of them. The hardcore leftist might even deny these implications, but they follow inexorably from the clear statements of materialism and naturalism.

As the old maxim goes, "If you say A, you must say B." That is, certain statements logically lead us to other statements, whether we like it or not. So if human life evolved from blind evolutionary processes, without guidance from a Creator, then

- Human life has no particular significance; humans, like other animals, are locked in a struggle for survival that has winners and losers.
- Government and its power are simply part of that struggle for survival in organized societies; those who have the power make the rules, and those who make the rules have advantages over those who don't.

- The ends justify the means, and the ends are decided solely by those in power.
- To say that people have a "right" to enjoy the benefits of their work, risks, and investment is no more logical than to say that a tiger has a "right" to enjoy an animal that it has killed. Because all creatures are engaged in a meaningless struggle for survival, nothing can or should stop a bigger tiger from taking over the kill and enjoying the fruits of the first tiger's labor. That's just the way the world works. And, in a similar vein, there is no moral prohibition against politicians using their power to transfer wealth from those who worked for it to those who voted for the politicians.

DO LEFTISTS REALLY BELIEVE SUCH THINGS?

Marxist intellectuals could not argue with the above statements. Those statements follow inevitably from the belief that human life is an accidental process and that our religious beliefs are merely "opiates" to help us cope with the hardness of life.

But how about American liberals, the philosophical descendants of European Marxism? Where would they stand on the above statements?

Hardcore liberals might want to deny them—at least in public— because otherwise they would forfeit their self-proclaimed moral superiority. But, no doubt, there are hardcore leftists who have fully considered the implications of their belief that the world and its inhabitants are the result of a cosmic accident. To them, lying about an opponent is permitted because everything is permitted.

But we want to be clear that you will meet liberals who spout the liberal worldview without having consciously subscribed to the *implications* of that worldview. For example, they might spout Darwinist rhetoric without ever really thinking through the implications of that rhetoric. Or they might claim that there are no absolute standards of right and wrong even as they insist that racism is morally evil, without ever stopping to consider the contradictions in those two statements.

For these leftists, it is the insatiable hunger for power over others that drives them into liberal politics. For them, the appeal of the liberal worldview is just its veneer of intellectual respectability.

But if liberals subscribe to Darwinism—and few things will get the panties of the average liberal in a twist like questioning Darwinism in public schools—then Darwinism has unavoidable implications, regardless of how we might feel about those implications. Because there is no path that takes us from "Darwin is right" to "poverty is wrong," for example, their proclamations about poverty must have some purpose other than curing poverty. Exposing that deeper purpose will be a powerful tool in the struggle against liberalism.

Furthermore, hardcore liberals are unlikely to admit to the possibility of any absolute standards of right and wrong, preferring instead the softer constraints of moral relativism. So though liberal hardliners might try to deny the implications of their positions on Darwinism, and their position that morality is nothing more than social habits, the implications are still there.

If you say A, you must say B. And when the implications are exposed, the left's most foundational beliefs on questions of origins and morality contradict the moral grandstanding that characterizes their public pronouncements. The better the mainstream can spot and expose the assumptions and beliefs that underlie most liberal positions, and the better we can point to the implications of those beliefs, the better we can defeat the left in politics.

The tactics we will teach in later chapters are designed to expose the left's underlying worldview and its implications, because uninformed and misinformed voters—who sometimes vote with the left—would be appalled at the implications of common liberal statements, if those implications were laid bare. Uninformed and misinformed liberal voters share many of the fundamental assumptions of the Judeo-Christian worldview and many of the character traits of mainstream America. But because they have been immersed in liberal dogma through the liberal institutions, these voters may espouse liberal viewpoints and vote for liberal policies without having consciously *converted* to the underlying worldview. Thus they can easily support "academic freedom," for example, while opposing the teaching of intelligent design, not because they are hypocrites, but because uninformed and misinformed liberals do not live and breathe politics. They simply do not take the time to explore the logical *implications* of the sweet-sounding liberal rhetoric, and so they would never see the contradictions between supporting academic freedom and opposing the teaching of intelligent design.

And, at the bottom of it all, it would most definitely never occur to the uninformed and misinformed that, if Darwin was right, then all the sweet liberal rhetoric they have absorbed is meaningless. How can racism be wrong and tolerance be good if Darwinism is right and we are nothing but chemical processes? Like it or not, if life resulted from chemical accidents, then there are just winners and losers in the big struggle.

Why should we help the poor or save the planet? How can there be economic justice or injustice in a world of species engaged in a meaningless struggle for survival? We might be put off if we see a cat eating a beautiful bird or an alligator eating a cat, but we could not say that the cat or the alligator had committed an injustice. If Darwin was right, some creatures survive and others do not.

If we really evolved from blind physical processes, then some people will just make out better than others in life, and so what? The fittest survive and thrive, and the devil take the hindmost. There's no need to get excited about any of it unless you happen to be one of the ones getting weeded out; and even then, once you die, everything just goes black forever. It was nothing personal.

Once we are unmoored from the idea that our existence and our worth comes from a Creator who is outside of Nature, we are logically compelled to follow the same path as earlier skeptics, and we end up at nihilism. A worldview that is founded on nothing can have nothing as a moral reference point.

It is telling that the hardcore left defends Darwinism with all the zeal and fervor of missionaries. Though their rhetoric lauds "open-mindedness" and "diversity," liberals censor any efforts to remind students that

Darwinism is a *theory* and not a gospel, or that respected scientists using sophisticated mathematics and the latest evidence from physics have concluded that life is too complex to have resulted from the accidental combinations of chemicals.[49]

Why this "religious" devotion on the left to this one particular theory? Why do liberals not panic when quantum mechanics threatens a Newtonian view of the world? Why do liberals not make a federal court case out of superstring theory? Why do liberals not take a fierce stand on the question of why gravity is so much weaker than the three other fundamental forces?

Maybe it is not science or the search for truth that hardcore liberals love about Darwin's theory; maybe what they love is the *implications* of his theory. If Darwin was right, then there is no right and wrong. There are only winners and losers. Some animals make it to the top of the heap and others don't, and maybe hardcore liberals just aim to be at the top of the heap.

If Darwin was right, then Nietzsche was right, and everything really *is* permitted.

Maybe all the lofty liberal rhetoric about science, equality, fairness, diversity, justice, children, the poor, and the elderly is just a means to an end.

So the question becomes: "What end?"

YOU SHALL BE AS GODS

Once the foundations of the liberal worldview are accepted as true, the liberal claim of moral superiority over the rest of us falls apart. If all standards are subjective and one is no better than the other, then by what standard is social justice better than social injustice? Why is equality better than discrimination? Why is it so important to "spread the wealth around"?

And why are the leftists who chant "Who are we to judge?" so darn judgmental?

THE LIBERAL PARADOX: DOGMATIC NIHILISM

The liberal worldview just seems to be inconsistent with left-wing preachiness. How can one be holier-than-thou if there is nothing holy? How can liberals, who constantly tell us that all values are subjective and relative, be so constantly dogmatic? The inconsistency seems dizzying.

But there is no inconsistency between the liberal worldview and changeable, arbitrary liberal standards. There is no liberal hypocrisy. Professed liberal standards such as tolerance and diversity only *seem* to conflict with liberal demands, such as censoring any speech they do not like.

Leftist "values" and leftist actions are perfectly consistent: At all times, and in all places, liberal moralizing merely serves the personal interests of the liberal. Tolerance is good when there is something that liberals want tolerated. Everything else violates the First Amendment. Diversity is good when the diversity serves liberal preferences. Everything else is hate speech.

Because their use of moral language is arbitrary and self-serving, true leftists seem to experience no guilt because, in their world, they are not being hypocritical. They can call their opposition racist while exploiting black Americans for their votes because both actions serve their own self-interest. They can dumb down our schools while accusing their opponents of not supporting education because both tactics work to the advantage of leftists.

These tactics have worked for years because mainstream Americans look in the wrong place for consistency. When we try to prove, using evidence and reason, that we don't hate the poor and we don't want to push Granny off a cliff, we are assuming that liberals actually believe their accusations, and that contradictory evidence will convince them that they are wrong. We have failed to see that the only consistency in liberal rhetoric is in the benefit of that rhetoric for the liberal.

In order to make sense of the dizzying array of contradictions in liberal rhetoric, however, all we need to do is to use liberal rhetoric from one situation to contradict liberal rhetoric in another. And when we do so, the *real* consistency emerges.

AN IMAGINARY DEBATE
WITH A LIBERAL ENVIRONMENTALIST

In other words, the way to defeat a leftist in a debate is to start from their worldview and follow the implications to their logical end. Don't waste your time arguing with hardcore liberals; just get hardcore liberals to argue with themselves. We will cover this tactic in more detail when we talk about our core tools for exposing liberal hypocrisy and putting liberals on the defensive. For now, let's just see where the technique takes us.

The following imaginary debate with a liberal environmentalist is an illustration only. If you use this technique with real liberals, be aware that they can get nasty and even violent when they don't get their way.

Also note that we are extending the discussion to make a point, and to have a little fun in the process, as you will see. In reality, you wouldn't get past the third or fourth statement before the liberal started calling you names or hitting you.

> LIBERAL: *"We have to stop global warming, so we have to cut down on carbon emissions. That means we'll have to make some huge sacrifices here in the United States and take our guidance from the UN, but we have no other choice if humans are to survive."*

The habitual mainstream response would be to try to point to evidence that global warming is a fraud or to question the claim that any observed "warming" is caused by human activity. All the liberal would hear is "Blah blah blah," and then the name-calling would start. But suppose our response followed these lines:

> MAINSTREAMER: *"Are you saying that human beings have some special significance? Don't you believe that we just evolved from blind physical processes?"*

We have simply used one liberal position to contradict another. The technique works because all liberal positions serve the immediate and arbitrary self-interest of the liberal, so those positions often contradict each other as the desires of the liberal change from one situation to the next. We just want to bring the underlying self-serving nature to the surface.

In the methods we will cover in later chapters, after you have rebutted one liberal position with another liberal position, you would use the moment of stunned silence to refocus the discussion onto a topic that you want to discuss and the liberal doesn't. But to make the point, let's continue along this line for a bit.

LIBERAL: *"Well, of course I believe that humans are the result of purely physical processes. Darwinism is a proven scientific fact. But what's that got to do with saving our species?"*

MAINSTREAMER: *"If Darwin is right, genetic mutations and natural selection will handle any climate changes. Those who adapt to the new climate will survive; those who don't, won't."*

LIBERAL: *"But humans have evolved the ability to reason through the process of natural selection, so now we can use that ability to save ourselves from extinction."*

MAINSTREAMER: *"If Darwin was right, species aren't trying to survive. They just have characteristics that either support survival or they don't. Maybe some humans will thrive if the climate warms and others won't, but that's not really the point. Species come and go. Most species that ever existed are extinct, aren't they? Why should that process stop now, just because we happen to be here? Global warming will just select some people and species for survival and others for extinction. I think you're imposing a moral standard on something that isn't a moral question."*

LIBERAL: *"Of course it's a moral question! We're talking about the future of the human species! Besides, Americans do the most damage to the planet because of our greedy economy, and poor people in other parts of the world suffer because of our greed and our destruction of the earth's resources and our carbon emissions and our warming of the planet. It's time that our government started righting some of these wrongs."*

MAINSTREAMER: *"It sounds like you're imposing your own value judgments on greed. In a diverse, multicultural world, different people will evolve different values, none of which is better or worse than any other. Greed is just a value that some people have and others don't. It's fine if you want to worry about poor people in other countries, but who's to say that others have to share your values?"*

LIBERAL: *"What kind of person are you? Are you defending greed? Don't you want to survive? Of course American greed is wrong and it's wrong to let poor people suffer. It's just not fair!"*

MAINSTREAMER: *"Sure I want to survive, but I don't think the planet will die from global warming before my time is up. So it won't affect me personally. And besides, who's to say that it's wrong for poor people to suffer? Suffering is a natural process. We may not personally like suffering, but that doesn't mean we should make moral judgments about it. Besides, helping the poor sounds like a religious value, and you know what a problem it is when religion works its way into public policy."*

LIBERAL: *"Helping the poor isn't a religious . . . Well, I mean, you don't have to be religious nut . . . Say, what's the matter with you? Don't you CARE???"*

MAINSTREAMER: *"I don't see how caring fits into our discussion. Different people care about different things in a diverse and multicultural society. Caring about the poor or the planet might feel good to you and me, but we can't impose our standards on other people."*

LIBERAL: *"That's it! You just said it! Stop global warming and cut your carbon emissions because caring feels good to you personally! We all have to find our own truth, our own good and bad. Caring feels good to you, so it's part of your truth, your personal experience of goodness."*

MAINSTREAMER: *"But driving my SUV also feels good to me, just like air-conditioning, having flush toilets, and using deodorant."*

LIBERAL: *"I've had it with you! People like you ought to be shot for what you're doing to this planet!!!"*

MAINSTREAMER: *"But I thought you didn't approve of guns."*

LIBERAL: *"Guns should be outlawed, and you and other global warming deniers ought to be put in some kind of camp where you can't do any more damage to the earth."*

MAINSTREAMER: *"You mean a camp like Guantánamo? Last week you said we should close Guantánamo. But then who are we to say whether putting people in camps is a good thing or a bad thing?"*

LIBERAL: *"I say putting people like you in camps is good and saving the planet is good and carbon emissions are bad and caring about the poor is good and you and your stupid SUV and your deodorant and your flush toilets are bad! That's who says what's good and what's bad, you greedy, racist, sexist, intolerant, hatemongering tea bagger!"*

MAINSTREAMER: *"Well, those are your opinions. But then who's the ultimate judge of what's good and what's bad?"*

LIBERAL: *"I'll tell you who's the judge of what's good and what's bad: I am, that's who. I am."*

OK, we had a little fun toward the end. And, of course, liberals would claim that we have set up a "straw man" in our imaginary debate. But go through it again statement by statement. Does the mainstreamer make any statements that do not naturally follow from common liberal positions? Do any of the liberal statements sound different from liberal statements we hear every day? They do not. All we have done is use common liberal positions to rebut other common liberal positions. And when we do so, the contradictions burst to the surface.

When we dig beneath the surface of liberal statements that seem nonsensical and hypocritical, we find an appalling and frightening consistency. The inconsistency between the liberals' nihilistic, relativistic rhetoric on the one hand and their dogmatic moralism on the other is only an apparent inconsistency. There is perfect consistency if we accept the idea that in the leftist worldview the individual is the ultimate judge of right and wrong. We don't expose that underlying assumption in our practical debates with liberals, however, because we fall into the trap of debating them on terms that they put forth about the topic in question. So we debate the science behind global warming, and liberals call us crackpots and deniers. But when we simply pull up common liberal positions from *other* discussions and use those in the *current* discussion, the implications of the leftist worldview are laid bare.

We have arrived at the cold, dark heart of the leftist worldview, the place where moral relativism collapses upon itself like a black hole.

THE GOD IN THE LIBERAL MIRROR

Liberals cannot have it both ways. If, as liberals constantly tell us, there are no absolute moral standards, if morals are socially constructed conventions, if human life is the result of blind physical processes, then all leftist pontificating about the way life should be is nothing more than personal preference. Whether individual liberals would consciously think of themselves as the ultimate judges of right and wrong is irrelevant. What is important is that their rhetoric leads inexorably to that conclusion.

As Erik von Kuehnelt-Leddihn pointed out in his classic *Leftism Revisited*,[50] nihilism leaves a vacuum, a "dangerous hunger" that must be satisfied. Two brutal "isms" of the twentieth century, Nazism and communism, both grew out of the naturalistic and nihilistic worldview. Both followed a stream of thought that rejected the Judeo-Christian worldview, which had been the bedrock of Western civilization for centuries. American liberalism is the direct descendant of that same worldview; Nazism and communism are its philosophical cousins.

As Erik von Kuehnelt-Leddihn argued, something does indeed fill the moral vacuum of nihilism. If people claim to believe that there is no ultimate standard of right and wrong, they will still find some standard, because no human being actually lives as if right and wrong don't exist. That's why no thief will condone having his things stolen. But since they say everything is subjective, nihilists turn to the only standard they know for sure: their own likes and dislikes. The nihilist creates a moral vacuum and then fills that vacuum with his own ego.

Leftists deny universal standards of right and wrong, and then they insist that the country and everyone in it must abide by standards that they set. So where do they get these standards to which they hold everyone else? Who or what is the source of these standards? Who or what is the ultimate judge of right and wrong?

The left's only answer that follows from their stated positions is "I AM."

All that is missing is the burning bush.

Take as a final example the statement by Barack Obama during the 2008 presidential campaign that "spreading the wealth around is good for everyone." Let's probe that statement to reveal the assumptions and beliefs that would lead someone to make it.

Another, more detailed way of expressing Obama's desire to spread the wealth around would be

> *"Tomorrow morning, over three hundred million Americans will get up and make choices. Some will do honest work and some will commit crimes. Some will go to school and study hard so that they can be better informed citizens and more employable in the future. Others will go to school to create disruption for others, and they will learn little. Some will save the money that they have earned; some will enjoy what their money can buy today. Some will sacrifice, take risks, and invest what they have in starting small businesses. Many of these will struggle; some will fail. Others will finally succeed after years of sacrifice, hard work, and risk. In short, millions of Americans will make billions of decisions tomorrow, and each decision will produce results, some good and some bad.*
>
> *Then I, Barack Hussein Obama, will judge the results of those billions of decisions made by millions of people. If those results do not please me,*

if those results do not meet the standard that I set, I will take from some and give to others until I am pleased, because it is my personal belief that spreading the wealth around is good for everyone."

It is no coincidence that Whittaker Chambers described the ultimate promise of communism as having been around since the beginning of the world: "Ye shall be as gods."[51]

5

TODDLERS, TANTRUMS, AND TYRANNY

CHARACTER MATTERS

Once we see that American liberalism has its philosophical roots in a rejection of the Judeo-Christian worldview, we can understand how liberal tactics such as intimidation and pitting one group against another follow naturally from that worldview. In the worldview that gave birth to hardcore liberalism, everything is permitted because there are no absolute standards of right and wrong. Life is all about deciding your own values and satisfying yourself.

But we have all known people who struggle with the idea of moral absolutes, or who have doubts about the existence of God, or who believe that Darwin's theory was basically right, but who still don't become hardcore liberals. They might describe themselves as agnostic, or they might say that good and evil are situational and not absolutes, but they don't go postal over someone saying a prayer before a football game, and they don't make a federal case at the sight of a cross in public. They just mind their own business and leave other people free to do the same. They accept as a fact of adult life that people will not always agree with them and that society is under no obligation to kowtow to their wishes, and they don't get legalistic about it.

In fact, there are people like Ayn Rand, who rejected the claims of Judeo-Christian religious teachings and yet adopted a small-government, libertarian political philosophy. So why do some people who doubt the Judeo-Christian worldview occupy themselves with work and hobbies that don't infringe on the liberty of their neighbors, while others become left-wing activists who devote their lives to an insatiable quest for power and domination?

We believe that the answer lies in the *character* of the person holding the worldview. We will see that there are underlying differences, not just between mainstream and liberal worldviews, but also between mainstream and liberal *character*. All of the dizzying inconsistencies between liberal rhetoric and liberal actions disappear once we see hardcore liberalism as the result of the nihilistic worldview we just described combined with a particular set of character traits.

It will become evident why the irate toddler and the schoolyard bully have much in common with the liberal politicians and activists trying to mold the country in their own image.

CHARACTER AND LIBERTY

In his outstanding book *The Liberal Mind: The Psychological Roots of Political Madness,* psychiatrist Dr. Lyle Rossiter details two common challenges that each of us faces in growing up.[52] One is the development of independence, the ability to be responsible for ourselves and for our actions. The other is learning to balance our independence with respect for the needs and rights of others, so that we learn to cooperate with others instead of manipulating them to meet our ends. The rules we learn for our behavior during this process form the basis of our childhood conscience and ultimately our character. Failure to meet these challenges leaves people more vulnerable to the false promises of liberalism.

Our Constitution was written for a moral people, as John Adams cautioned us. But our Constitution was also intended for a psychologically *mature* people, as maturity is described in Rossiter's book. The Constitution assumes that citizens are capable of being independent, of taking care of themselves and their obligations, and consequently it provides for a high degree of liberty.

The Constitution also assumes that citizens are mature enough to cooperate *voluntarily* in order to meet certain shared goals, and that otherwise they are free to mind their own business. That's why the Constitution uses checks and balances as barriers to any minority who would try to coerce others to do their will. Only those measures that have broad-based support and mutual benefit are supposed get past those built-in barriers. This principle is at the heart of the belief that the power of government rests on the consent of the governed.

We have seen why the left has such disdain for our Constitution and our Judeo-Christian culture: Both are barriers to their ability to impose their will upon us. But liberal disdain for our republican system runs even deeper. People who are emotionally mature will resist government's intrusion into their lives, regardless of their worldview. So the left's political strategy has been to use our own cultural institutions to undermine not only our Judeo-Christian culture but also the development of mature character in our children and our citizens.

An emotionally immature and dependent population, one with a sense of resentful entitlement, makes a solid political base for the left. The promise that "I'll take care of you and punish your enemies" resonates with those who have failed to achieve independence and responsibility for themselves. That is why liberal tactics are designed to stoke resentment and encourage dependency in order to expand the left's power base.

THE DEVELOPMENT OF CHARACTER

In order to understand the bullying tactics of the left and why the mainstream majority has tolerated them, mainstream activists need a new way of thinking about common differences between mainstream and liberal character. Only when we change our understanding can we recognize the futility of traditional mainstream approaches to dealing with liberal tactics.

It should go without saying that in a book on political strategy and tactics, any discussion of character development will be simplified and generalized, as was our summary of the intellectual foundations of the Judeo-Christian and leftist worldviews. No doubt our thinking below will leave out many details, and we realize that our assessment will not apply to every individual in the mainstream or on the far left.

But mainstream America is not trying to pass a psychology test or a philosophy test. We are trying to save our republic from the Long March of the radical left. The patterns we describe below will be familiar enough to shed light on the dynamics behind the Appeasement Cycle. Our goal is to provide enough understanding of those dynamics to enable the mainstream to use more effective methods in saving our republic.

Tiny Tyrants

We are all born liberal, but most of us outgrow it. That is, we come into this world helpless and dependent. Some things feel good and we coo or laugh. Other things feel bad and we cry or scream with rage. We have no moral standards beyond our likes and dislikes. As infants, we have no sense of other people as people. They are just objects that respond to our needs, not fellow human beings with needs and rights of their own. We are the center of a world that seems to revolve around our urges and needs.

The difference between the crying newborn and the adult liberal is the protest sign and list of demands. Both are saying, in essence, "The ruckus will go on until you do what I want you to do." But, of course, the newborn is too young to know any better.

And newborns are cute.

GROWING GOOD CITIZENS

As we describe it in our model of development, the path from this helpless and dependent state to mature citizenship is a long one, and there are many things to learn in a few short years. A critical role of parents and caretakers and of our cultural institutions is to teach us that the world does not revolve around us, that our needs do not trump the rights of others, and that we must be responsible for ourselves.

Thus, good parenting and healthy cultural institutions help solve three major problems that all developing children confront:

1. *How do we behave so that we fit in socially?* Humans are social creatures. We live and work in families, tribes, villages, cities, and other social groups. Being able to fit in, to belong and get along with others, is essential to our survival.

2. *How do we develop some degree of independence, so that others are free to live their own lives without having to respond to our every need?* An important indicator of maturity is the ability to take care of oneself and to be responsible for one's own actions, emotions, and circumstances.

3. *How do we find the right balance between independence—doing things our own way—and living in relative harmony with others?* A state of total social independence would create chaos and constant conflict. My desire to listen to my music at a volume of my choosing would run into your desire not to listen to my music at all. Mature individuals have to find a balance between getting along with others and doing things our own way.

In essence, if we are to become good citizens, we must first learn what it takes to be good children. But how do parents teach us to be good before we are old enough to comprehend what "good" is? They can either watch over us every minute to keep us out of trouble, or they can take advantage of the brain's design and shape our behavior emotionally, which turns out to be much more efficient.

BELONGING AND REJECTION

Human beings are wired biologically to need approval and acceptance. Bonding means survival for infants and small children who cannot care for themselves independently. Our brains, like those of other mammals, respond to isolation from our loved ones by producing sensations of loneliness and discomfort. We see evidence of this in the whimpering of a puppy that has been separated from its litter, or the tears of a toddler when the babysitter arrives and his parents leave.

Our brains react not just to physical isolation but also to emotional isolation, that is, to disapproval and rejection. We see the power of social isolation in the pouting lip of the toddler who has been scolded. Disapproval works in the brain in much the same ways as physical abandonment, in that it creates very uncomfortable emotional states in us. This aspect of the brain's design enables parents to shape our behavior when we are too young to comprehend what is good for us and what might hurt or even kill us. Until we are old enough to contemplate what is *truly* good, our experience of "good" is simply that which makes others happy with us.

As we grow up, we learn that certain behaviors result in praise, affirmation, and approval from those around us, and we experience pleasant emotions. We experience ourselves as good children. We also learn that other behaviors result in scolding or disapproval, which trigger unpleasant emotions like guilt, fear, and sadness. When we get scolded, when others are angry with us, when we disappoint others, we experience ourselves as bad children.

None of this requires advanced training in the behavioral sciences to understand. The look on the face of a child who has been praised or scolded tells us all we need to know about the power of these emotional controls.

Over time, our social network grows beyond that of parents and family, and our interactions with others become more complicated, but the need for social belonging and safety remains. Underneath it all is a simple, built-in biological need: the need to be accepted and to belong. We move past the need to be fed and on to the need to be accepted, to fit in, to experience approval, to have a place in the family, the tribe, the village, or the team. This need is rooted in our biology, in the chemical processes that occur in our brains.

Some of us have a little more of this need for acceptance and are very tuned in to the feelings of others around us; others have a little less of it and test the social boundaries a little more. Anyone with children knows this. But we all have this basic social need or we wouldn't survive. Our need for approval and our desire to avoid rejection support our survival in a surprising way: These are the basis for our earliest conscience.

If all goes well, we learn some basic rules for fitting in, such as

- Mind your manners and be polite.
- Cooperate and get along with others.
- Don't be angry, bossy, or whiny.
- Respect the feelings of others.
- Follow the rules.
- Be fair.

INDEPENDENCE, POWER, AND HELPLESSNESS

There is a second problem that children have to solve, one that sometimes creates conflict with the need for approval. Keeping others happy helps us to avoid rejection, but it keeps us dependent on them as well. There are things we want to do and explore, and we don't want to have to get permission every time. In short, we like to be able to get our way.

And so a second problem arises: How do we become independent, able to do things that we want without having to rely on others? How can we gain an acceptable degree of power and control over our environment and, in some ways, over the people in our environment? That is, how do we behave in order to influence our environment and the people in it to do things the way we want?

Much of child development involves overcoming the helplessness of infancy and establishing some degree of independence. That's why we so often hear young children say, "I did it all by myself!" We learn to feed ourselves, to walk and become mobile, to tie our own shoes, and in countless other ways we are driven to show that we can do things ourselves. The visceral sense of pleasure is evident on the face of a young child who masters a new task for the first time, when we hear the triumphant, "Look at me!"

If all goes well, we learn some basic rules for developing independence, such as

- Take care of your own stuff.
- The more you can do for yourself, the better.
- Clean up your own messes.
- Learn from your mistakes.

WHAT'S YOURS IS YOURS AND WHAT'S MINE IS MINE

As noted above, these two major needs, the need for acceptance and the need for independence, create a new problem for us to solve. The more we assert our independence and do what we want to do, the more likely we are to encounter disapproval from others who wanted us to do something else. On the other hand, if we focus too much on doing what others want us to do in order to keep them happy, we sense that we have surrendered our independence.

At the core of this conflict is the issue of power. We want to have power over our own lives, our own decisions, and our own surroundings. But in order to get along peacefully with others, we have to accept some limits on our own power. Our solution to this conflict has political implications, because politics is all about power. As Rossiter emphasizes in *The Liberal Mind,* mature individuals minimize the use of coercive power by relying on voluntary cooperation wherever possible.

When we cooperate voluntarily with others, we do not impose our will on them or have their wills imposed on us. We mind our own business and leave others free to do the same, and then we voluntarily cooperate—when it is in our mutual interest to do so.

We might not *want* to pay taxes, but we do so because we have agreed that *some* level of taxation is important to pay for things that are to our mutual benefit, such as securing our borders. On the other hand, it is none of our business what radio station others listen to or which doctor they choose, and we expect other mature individuals to reciprocate that "live and let live" approach.

And that is part of the genius of our Constitution. The checks and balances, separation of powers, and the role of government all set a clear standard. The power of government will be used *only* when there is widespread agreement that it is in our mutual interest for government to act.

"Good Enough" Parenting

As Rossiter explains in *The Liberal Mind*, when children have "good enough" parenting, they should grow up with reasonable capacities for independence and for voluntary cooperation with others. Raising a child is complicated, and it's not possible to do a perfect job. Fortunately, a "good enough" job will work fine.

As Rossiter explains, "good enough" parenting is not abandoning and abusive. Children need to know that they are loved and valued, which is not surprising. But in a finding that might come as a surprise to many parents today, "good enough" parenting is not fawning or excessively protective. "Good enough" parenting does not include an obsessive quest for self-esteem or insulation from the normal frustrations of life. After all, children need to learn that they have rights, but that other people have rights too. Children need to learn that everything they touch will not turn to gold, that others do not owe them a living, and how to cope with that reality in mature ways.

In other words, regardless of the technological method that we use, children need to learn the wisdom that was captured in those early copybooks.

Think of growing up as learning to ride a bicycle. Early on in the process, "good enough" parents are like the training wheels that provide just enough support to avoid serious injury while getting the child through the wobbly phase. When there is abuse or abandonment, it is as if the emotional training wheels are not there to allow the child to learn to ride in reasonable safety. It's either ride or get hurt. These children experience failure and pain with little guidance as to how to overcome it. They learn that the world is a threatening place, and they lack the basic guidance necessary to meet the challenges of life on their own. As a means of coping with a frightening world, they learn to treat others as objects to prop them up instead of as people with feelings and rights of their own. Often they learn to manipulate and bully in order to get what they want from other people.

But in the case of fawning and pampering parents, it is as if the emotional training wheels are never removed. The support and praise are always there, regardless of what the child does. Such pampering does *not* result in a truly confident child, because the child never learns to handle the normal frustrations of life. The child may appear confident on the surface, but that confidence is shallow; it depends on the ongoing adoration and support of others. The child learns to expect that others will always clean up after him. The child does not learn to handle setbacks and disappointments in a mature manner. The child learns that the world will kowtow to his every whim, and that he is entitled to what he wants, when he wants it. When the world doesn't kowtow, the child learns to turn up the emotional heat until others give in.

"Good enough" parenting provides discipline without abuse, and love without spoiling the child. But without the solid grounding of "good enough" parenting, children learn to seek safety and reassurance by manipulating and bullying others to meet the needs that they cannot meet themselves. The child learns that he is helpless to meet his own needs on the one hand, or that he should not have to on the other. And when such children see independence and success in others, they often feel shame, envy, and resentment.

Absent a major change in the development of their character, such children would be easy prey for the envy, resentment, and entitlement preached by the far left.

"Good Enough" Cultural Institutions

Parents have tremendous influence, particularly on small children, but that influence becomes more and more limited as the child moves through the institutions of our culture. By age six, most children spend more of their waking hours in a school run by the government than with their parents. You often hear as an explanation for the pitiful academic results of our schoolchildren that the schools are being asked to make up for the failings of the parents. But we believe that the bigger concern, given the liberal domination of our educational system, is that the schools undermine the efforts of parents who are trying to do a "good enough" job of parenting.

If our institutions shared the mainstream worldview, those institutions would reinforce the values and habits taught by mainstream parents. Children would learn the balance between getting their own way and respecting the rights of others. They would learn that achievement is not free. They would learn that self-discipline is a prerequisite for self-esteem, and that self-esteem is not the highest good in the universe.

What happens, however, when the parents provide "good enough" parenting, but the social institutions that surround the child undermine that parenting? What if the cultural institutions teach effortless success, immediate gratification, entitlement, and resentment for the success of others? What if those institutions teach children that if they don't have what they want, someone else has done them dirty? What if parents attempt to teach self-discipline and culture teaches self-esteem instead?

Though parents have a tremendous impact on the development of their children's character, cultural institutions can either support or undermine what the parents teach. The cultural Marxists knew what they were doing when they targeted the traditional family as a barrier to their plans.

WORLDVIEW AND CONSCIENCE

We often speak of the childhood conscience as *visceral*, as a physical feeling in the gut that one has done something right or wrong. The childhood conscience serves its purpose when we are too young to truly understand right and wrong.

As we mature, however, we begin to develop our worldview, as we described in the last chapter. We begin to wonder where we came from and where we're going, and we begin to ask ourselves how we should behave along the way. We begin to consider questions of right and wrong behavior that do not depend on making others happy with us or on feeling good about ourselves. We begin to develop a worldview that does not revolve around our own likes and dislikes. In short, we begin to exhibit the workings of an adult conscience.

Furthermore, as we mature, we begin to understand what it feels like when someone hits us, or takes our belongings, or makes us do things that we don't want to do. And we begin to realize that others have similar experiences if we hit them, or take their belongings, or make them do things that they don't want to do. We take a huge step toward maturity when we realize that other people do not exist to serve us; they have feelings and rights just as we do. For mainstream Americans, the Golden Rule takes shape in some form in our minds.

The adult conscience often lacks the emotional intensity of the childhood conscience, which is almost all visceral. We might think of the adult conscience as the "still, small voice" described by the prophet Elijah, the voice that convicts us when we have treated someone else in a way that we would not want to be treated, the voice telling us that we are not, in fact, the center of the universe, that our whims are not the ultimate standard of right and wrong.[53]

Our childhood conscience is the result of immersion; our adult conscience is the result of conversion, of a more conscious and deliberate choice. If we were raised in a Judeo-Christian culture, then our adult conscience will extend and amplify the visceral messages of the childhood conscience. The childhood conscience might trigger guilt and sadness if we get angry and behave rudely with someone else, but our adult conscience would also tell us in a quieter way that we have not done as we should have done. The childhood conscience *feels bad* because the other person is hurt or angry and disappointed with us, and we have a deep-seated rule that we should feel bad if others are unhappy with us. But the adult conscience tells us we have *done wrong*, in the sense of violating a standard that we have accepted as true.

In this case, the childhood conscience adds some emotional fire to the more abstract adult conscience, and we feel motivated to make amends.

KNOWING RIGHT BUT FEELING WRONG

In order to fully grasp how the mainstream majority gets dominated by the liberal minority, we need to look at what happens when our early messages, the visceral or "gut" ones, conflict with our more adult sense of right and wrong. We have all experienced times when we *know* a particular course of action is right but we still feel guilty or otherwise miserable about doing it. Maybe we know intellectually that laying employees off now will save the company and protect those jobs that remain. One part of us *knows* we have to do the layoffs and that the layoffs are morally justified in order to save other jobs, and yet another part of us *feels* guilty and sad because people will suffer. In these cases, we can say that the adult and childhood consciences are sending us different messages.

Please do not think that this conflict as necessarily a bad thing. A manager who does the layoffs because it is the right thing to do but feels sadness and guilt afterward is simply a mature human being. Sometimes life is complicated, and we don't get to feel good just because we do the right thing. We might be at peace with the rightness of our actions intellectually, but we can still feel the lingering unpleasantness in our gut. So we have to cowboy up and do the right thing even if it doesn't feel good, because that's just what grown-ups do.

THE ROOTS OF THE APPEASEMENT CYCLE

All of this works well enough when we're dealing with other people who share our Judeo-Christian culture and whose character has developed along the same lines as ours. We can resolve most social conflicts by voluntary cooperation, and compromise is often acceptable because we are all playing from the same moral rulebook. Explanations, evidence, and reasoning, all used within an atmosphere of mutual courtesy and respect, work well enough and enough of the time to become habits in handling differences among mainstream Americans.

But serious problems arise when we are dealing with people who failed to develop a respect for the needs and rights of other people. These people are more concerned about what feels good to them than about what is socially acceptable. Compound this emotional immaturity with a worldview that says "everything is permitted" and you have everything you need to make a hardcore leftist.

Two Common Character Patterns

Two common patterns are especially important for understanding the difference between mainstream Americans and liberal hardliners. In terms of political inclinations, we can think of these two character types as Good Citizens and Power Players. Of course, these would be too simplistic to be valuable as personality types, but if we remember that these are *political* types, then the essential struggle going on in America today will come into sharp focus.

GOOD CITIZENS

As children, Good Citizens learn that they should do their best to get along with others. They seek harmony, agreement, and acceptance in their social world to the extent possible. As all children do, they have a mischievous side, and they are far from little angels, but a major theme in their life centers around being responsible and getting along reasonably well with others.

Good Citizens have needs for power and control, but those needs get channeled into productive activity in school, work, sports, hobbies, and, later, in taking care of their families and other adult responsibilities. Of course, Good Citizens like to get their way, but this normal desire is bounded by the Golden Rule. There are social boundaries that they know not to cross in the effort to get their way.

Conflict with others is, of course, inevitable, but Good Citizens dislike conflict for the most part and try to minimize it whenever possible. They rely on standards of fairness to resolve conflicts, and they will compromise when it's necessary to keep the peace.

If they do something wrong, they experience a visceral sense of guilt as well as the "still, small voice" guiding them in the right direction. The visceral need for social harmony is so deeply ingrained in the childhood consciences of these Good Citizens that they often feel pangs of guilt for taking actions that they knew in their adult consciences were the right actions.

For some, the visceral discomfort with conflict is strong enough that they often back down to keep the peace, even when they know that they are right. They dread the schoolyard bully, the irate customer, the thin-skinned family member, and the difficult co-worker because of the potential for conflict, and they sometimes find avoidance and appeasement to be more comfortable in the short run than dealing with the verbal abuse that these social tyrants can dish out.

In their private lives, Good Citizens suffer all the foibles and shortcomings that come with being human. They are far from perfect, and they know it. But their public, political lives are for the most part defined by a willingness to mind their own business and let others do the same.

Good Citizens who are politically involved are far more likely to be conservative than liberal. Good Citizens who are liberal have typically been immersed in liberal rhetoric by the cultural institutions, and they have taken that rhetoric at face value. Because they do not live and breathe politics, these Good Citizen liberals do not think through the implications of liberal positions.

POWER PLAYERS

For reasons varying from genetics to parenting to the influence of cultural institutions, we see another political character type in people who have difficulty gaining independence in childhood. Perhaps some did not get enough parental support, maybe others were pampered, and maybe still others had parents who did a good enough job that was undermined by leftist influences in the culture.

However it happened, without an adequate foundation of self-confidence and independence, these people too often must rely on others to meet many of their physical or emotional needs. But they find that others who have developed a sense of independence become less and less willing to step into the role of provider and comforter for them as they grow older. As a result, the Power Players learn ways of manipulating others into those provider and comforter roles. Sometimes the manipulation is subtle, such as presenting themselves as helpless victims and trying to elicit pity and guilt. At other times the manipulation is more overt, complete with flashes of anger, threats, and bullying. Because of their dependency on others, Power Players tend to see others as objects to be manipulated rather than as fellow human beings with needs and rights of their own.

Though they may be capable of charm, social harmony is less important to Power Players than getting their way, and their anger surges to the surface when they are frustrated. The success of others appears to trigger in them shame, bitterness, and envy instead of serving as inspiration.

Struggling desperately to find a sense of their own worth, Power Players have difficulty recognizing the worth of others. If their manipulation creates stress and misery for other people, that is just the price that has to be paid for getting their way, for dominating whatever relationships or groups to which they belong.

When they experience a threat to their sense of being powerful, Power Players experience visceral fears of weakness, inadequacy, and being unimportant. Good Citizens having the same experiences of failure and embarrassment learn to try harder or to change their strategies in order to avoid repeating those experiences. Power Players, however, are more likely to turn up the heat on their manipulation and bullying of others.

The air of moral and intellectual superiority of liberalism soothes the inner fears and frustrations of the Power Players. And the denial of the Judeo-Christian worldview offers an even more tempting benefit in that it allows them to justify their behavior with an appeal to moral relativism.

Others may try to rescue or placate Power Players in an attempt to mollify these social bullies. But no amount of concession or approval seems to make any difference. Power Players are desperately struggling to become the center of a universe that stubbornly refuses to revolve around them.

This is the pattern that we see among the hardcore left. The insatiable lust for power and control and the willingness to bully and manipulate others all stem from failure to find appropriate ways of meeting their own needs and to respect the rights of others to do the same.

FROM POWER PLAYER TO HARDCORE LEFTIST

As we have said, the worldview that underlies American liberalism came through the worldview of Friedrich Nietzsche: God is dead; everything is permitted. And the character that underlies American liberalism is the self-centered character of the very young child around whom the world revolves.

But why are the Power Player characters drawn to *liberal* politics instead of just to politics in general? After all, politics is the world of power, and these characters live and breathe power. Couldn't they satisfy that need by becoming conservative politicians?

The answer is that liberal politics, despite its feel-good rhetoric, is about expanding government, and that means expanding power. Aside from moral traditions that are widely shared, conservative political views do not lend themselves to meddling in the lives of others. Liberal political views, however, provide the perfect cover for those with desperate needs to manipulate and bully others. That is why Power Players gravitate toward liberal politics.

When we listen past the holier-than-thou rhetoric of the left, when we listen past the rage and accusations at their demonstrations, we hear the unmistakable whine of the frustrated toddler: "But I *want* it!"

Every seeming contradiction between liberal rhetoric and liberal actions disappears when we understand the Three Commandments of Liberalism:

I. If I like it, it is good.
II. If I don't like it, it is bad.
III. Thou shalt not thwart my will.

The first two commandments derive from the denial of any external standards of right and wrong. The third derives from the insatiable hunger for power that characterizes Power Players. The liberal double standards about race, wealth, tolerance, diversity, education, and all the other shibboleths can be seen for what they are: fanfare to cover their real agenda.

WHY GOOD CITIZENS LOSE AT POLITICS

Mainstream Americans try to get along with others in harmony, as long as it is up to us to do so. When others are angry or disappointed with us, we feel discomfort both viscerally and intellectually. That is, our childhood conscience tells us that it is *bad* to make others unhappy, and our adult conscience tells us that we should treat others the way we would be treated. We don't like others to do things that create problems for us, and we try not to create problems for others.

Let's look at a simple scenario as a metaphor for what has happened in American politics. Imagine five mainstream Americans on the board of a local health club as they discuss plans for the future. Some board members want to pave the extra parking lot out of concern that senior citizens might have trouble walking on the gravel. Others mention that the room used by the cardiac care class is crowded and needs to be remodeled. Still others point out the expense involved in those projects and remind the board that the costs could drive up membership fees, and higher fees might be a hardship for younger members with families.

Now think of your experience in similar family, civic, and work situations, in which others share your basic concerns and play from the same social rulebook. One of those "rules" is that we should offer facts and evidence in support of our ideas. Another is that we should realize that our perspectives may be limited or biased, so we should be open to evidence, facts, and reason from others. And we are trying to make decisions that are best for all. "Reaching across the aisle" to the other side in these situations makes sense because we all want to do what is right and fair for the group as a whole.

WHY WE FIGHT THE WRONG BATTLE

But here is the critical question that sheds light on the Appeasement Cycle and the success of the liberal Long March through our institutions: What if one of the five members on the board is a Power Player? And what if that Power Player simply wants to funnel money to a relative in the paving business, and he hides that agenda underneath lofty rhetoric about elderly people struggling in a gravel parking lot? What if those relatives will return the favor in the form of extravagant "birthday presents" for their benefactor, the cost of which will be included in the paving contract?

As a Good Citizen, you listen to the expressed concerns about the gravel lot, and you notice some holes in the argument. You assume that the other side would want to know where their concerns might be misplaced, because you would want to know if your concerns were misplaced. So, first off, you point out that the gravel lot is only used for spillover parking, and it is rarely used even for that. Second, you mention that there have been no member complaints about the gravel lot, but there have been numerous concerns about rising fees. Finally, you note that the proposed paving contract seems exorbitant, especially in a weak economy in which paving companies should be hungry for business.

Despite these sensible arguments, you will have accomplished nothing. All of your reasoning, facts, and evidence will have been worse than useless because you were working from a flawed assumption that the other side in the debate was actually concerned about the elderly, the gravel parking lot, and getting the best paving contract for the good of all. It will not matter a hill of beans that your arguments were powerful and right. All the Power Player will hear is that you are standing in his way.

Let's continue with our health club example, though it should be clear by now that we are talking about the pattern we see every day in our national politics. Imagine the Power Player starts to make snarky comments about how "some of the younger members of the board" don't seem to care about the elderly members. You point out that your parents are elderly and you want to treat the elderly right, but you are still not convinced that there is a problem with the gravel lot.

Now imagine that the Power Player produces a letter from one of the elderly members of the club complaining about almost falling on the gravel, maybe even suggesting the possibility of litigation if the "gravel-lot crisis" isn't addressed immediately. You notice that the person who wrote the letter is a member of the family that owns the paving company, so you mention that. Instead of addressing your legitimate concern, however, the Power Player comes at you with vitriol. "How can you be so heartless? Don't you care about the elderly? Well, by golly, the right attorney just might *make* you care."

You look out the window, and on the sidewalk in front of the health club are a small number of angry, loud protesters, carrying signs demanding that the gravel-lot crisis be solved immediately. You notice that they all seem to have arrived in a van owned by the paving business that wants the contract.

All the other Good Citizens on the board are getting visibly uncomfortable, and now something really strange happens. Even though the rest of the board members share your concerns, and even though the four of you outnumber the single Power Player, some of the other Good Citizens suggest that you might want to ease up a bit. "Of course you've made some good points here, but is it really worth all this rancor? We all have to get along, after all. Maybe we can work something out."

Why do they pressure you to back down instead of pressuring the Power Player, who is obviously trying to funnel money to a family member and who is making life on the board miserable for everyone else? Because you won't raise a ruckus if you don't get your way and the Power Player will.

And so the Good Citizens "reach across the aisle" to the Power Player with a compromise: Let's just pave half of the gravel lot this year. The Power Player agrees. But it's not over—the Power Player also has relatives in the roofing business. On and on it goes. This is how the Appeasement Cycle works; this is how the 20 percent of the far left manipulate the rest of us.

And this is how the United States got a $15 trillion debt.

HOW LIBERALS USE OUR CIVILITY TO RULE US

How many times do you hear mainstream politicians on television trying to prove that the Tea Party is not racist, that some psychotic's violent rampage was not caused by talk radio, or that they don't want to push Granny off a cliff or starve innocent children?

And how many times do you hear the "voices of moderation" suggesting that maybe the Tea Party might be a little extreme, that we all have to "work together to get things done"? And why do those "voices of moderation" call on the mainstream to get along? Because they are afraid of displeasing the radical left and they are not afraid of displeasing the mainstream. Because those "voices of moderation" know the mainstream doesn't have the stomach for protracted political unpleasantness and that the radical left does.

Mainstream Americans fall into the Appeasement Cycle for two reasons. One is that we naïvely believe that reasoning, evidence, and facts will eventually convince the left of the damage caused by their social policies. And when all of our reasoning proves futile and the left turns to anger and accusations, we do what Good Citizens do and try to find common ground.

The second reason is that our adult conscience may tell us that we are in the right, but our childhood conscience is still uncomfortable with conflict, because buried in that childhood conscience is the belief that if others are angry with us, it is because we have done something wrong. This is not a conscious belief. It is stored deep inside our brains in the form of habits that we learned as part of becoming good children. It takes the form of the "butterflies" in our stomachs when there is tense conflict at home or at work or in politics.

And anger is the signature emotion of those on the radical left. Unable to find comfort in their own skin, they lash out at others in a desperate attempt to manipulate them into providing the comfort that they seek. They sense our desire for peace and harmony, just as a toddler senses that parents do not want to be embarrassed in a toy store.

Liberal accusations and demands trigger our deep dread of disapproval and conflict. Even when our rational brains and adult conscience tell us we are in the right, we have a nagging sense of threat down in our gut. We try in vain to explain ourselves and to educate the liberal, but, all too often, we appease in an attempt to make peace. Each time we appease, we make the next attack more likely.

And liberals always come back for more. No amount of meddling, coercing, demanding, or controlling can give them the emotional peace they so desperately seek. The hole inside of them is a result of their worldview. The hole inside of them is a spiritual one, and it cannot be filled with earthly power.

The Appeasement Cycle has brought power to the radical left, but it has not yet brought them peace. The world will never be the way they want it. The world will never kowtow to their every demand. But that hasn't stopped them from trying. And it has brought a loss of liberty and trillions of dollars in debt for the mainstream.

To break the Appeasement Cycle, mainstream America will have to confront our fear of conflict and disapproval. We will have to find something inside of us that is more powerful than our desire for social harmony.

6

A POLITICAL STRATEGY FOR MAINSTREAM AMERICA

The superiority of our ideas will do nothing to restore legitimacy to our government until mainstream America realizes that politics is about getting and using power. Only those who understand power get to put their ideas into practice. And, as we have argued, just being good citizens who vote is not a path to real political power.

Classical Marxists focused on controlling the means of production as the source of political power. Cultural Marxists revised this thinking and focused on controlling the cultural institutions. Because they have gained control of our educational, news, and other cultural institutions, the radical left can define the Tea Party as "extremist" and SEIU mobs as "democracy in action."

The popular term for this kind of control over the national discussion is "controlling the narrative," and reclaiming control of that narrative from the left will be the centerpiece of our new strategy. To carry out our strategy, the mainstream will have to stop thinking like outsiders in our own country and start thinking and acting like the political giant that we are.

Not only do mainstream Americans have to become political

activists, we also have to treat every day as if it were the day before election day.

GOALS OF A MAINSTREAM POLITICAL STRATEGY

We offer the following as a summary of a new political strategy for mainstream Americans:

To control the formal power of government by dominating the culture and the cultural institutions that determine the political narrative.

Put another way, mainstream America needs to launch our own Long March through the culture and the cultural institutions so that political debates occur on terms decided by the mainstream and not those set by the political left. Note that we target the broader culture, including day-to-day informal discussions, as well as the cultural institutions such as news, education, and entertainment.

Much of the political narrative occurs in casual conversations in the office, at work, at church, around the dinner table, and at other informal gatherings. It will take much longer for our strategy to affect the formal cultural institutions such as schools and news media, but we can begin to change the direction and tone of the political narrative outside of those institutions. In fact, we can undermine the results of the left's control of the formal institutions by taking control of the narrative downstream from those institutions, in those countless informal settings that they do not yet control.

Obviously we will not get all mainstream Americans on board with this strategy, nor is that necessary. Our numerical advantage over the left is so overwhelming that we can defeat them handily if we change our tactics.

To achieve our strategic goal, we will need to achieve three essential tactical goals. The remainder of this book will cover principles and tools for achieving these tactical goals. But just remember: isolate, dominate, and educate. Every principle and all of the tools we will cover are designed to achieve one or more of the following goals.

ISOLATE THE RADICAL LEFT

Put simply, we need to reveal the radicalism and arrogance behind all the sweet "progressive" language. We need to create the impression in our culture that leftist thinking is odd thinking. Harsh as it may sound, we will only be successful when liberalism is seen as ludicrous, not only among the 40 percent of the electorate who are conservative but also among the swing voters who are currently uninformed or misinformed.

We will know we are winning when Tina Fey can only get laughs by impersonating Nancy Pelosi instead of Sarah Palin. Just imagine:

Tina Fey as Pelosi: Each month that we don't have a stimulus bill, five hundred million Americans lose their jobs. [Audience chuckles and groans.] And I can see them all from the Mother Ship. [Audience erupts in laughter.]

Humor can be deadly serious in politics. When liberals sense that they are seen as humorous instead of as intimidating, they will turn up the volume. So be it. The more vocal they get, the more their true nature will be exposed for all to see, especially the uninformed and misinformed swing voters. Liberal credibility will suffer, as it should.

And leftist confidence will suffer. An old rule of combat is to take away the enemy's will to fight. When liberal dogma leads to embarrassment and a sense of being isolated from the mainstream of public thought, liberals will be far less likely to push their dogma. In order to defeat liberalism, we have to first take the wind out of liberal sails. We want them to shrug their shoulders and say, "What's the point?" when they are invited to a demonstration or a dead voter registration drive.

Right now, leftists typically leave encounters with the mainstream thinking something like, "Well, I guess I really showed them! I bet they're feeling pretty stupid right now." They experience themselves as powerful, as intellectually and morally superior. From now on, when they leave encounters with the mainstream, we want them thinking things like, "Whoa. That didn't work out the way I planned it."

If that sounds harsh, remember that this is politics, not civics. Attitude is a large part of winning in any endeavor, and we need to replace the confidence and arrogance of the hardcore left with doubt, hesitation, embarrassment, and a sense of political isolation.

And we want our target audience, the uninformed and misinformed who sometimes give liberals the majority at the polls, to start seeing the left as isolated and far outside of the mainstream of American thinking.

Dominate the Political Narrative

In the mainstream we have been so busy defending ourselves against liberal initiatives that we've become accustomed to being on the defensive. The left controls the political narrative, they define the terms of the debate, and then we try to defend ourselves within those boundaries.

The left has dumbed down our news and educational systems to serve their political agenda. Obviously we need to educate the uninformed and misinformed in order to take our culture back, but that will take time, and we cannot have the political discourse we need with the constant racket coming from the far left. It's like trying to give singing lessons in a sawmill.

The hardest part of our strategy for the mainstream to accept will be the need to put the left on the defensive, to keep them so busy fighting off our accusations and initiatives that they have no time or resources to mount their own. Politically pushing other people into a corner is just not in the nature of the mainstream. But the left has shown us that they will not leave us in peace, and they will not stop until they have total control over every aspect of our lives.

With liberals, you either dominate them or they dominate you. There can be no middle ground.

EDUCATE THE UNINFORMED AND MISINFORMED

We can't consistently win formal power with only the 40 percent of voters who describe themselves as conservative. Wherever possible, we want our methods to educate the uninformed and misinformed voters who often vote based on what they hear from cultural institutions. Right now, we pull enough of those voters to our side to win occasional victories at the polls. What we need is a permanent and solid conservative majority, one in which leftist ideas have trouble taking root.

When we expose the *real* message behind liberal accusations and demands, most uninformed and misinformed voters will smell hypocrisy, and that is a huge turnoff in politics. Discrediting the left is a critical short-term goal. As long as the left loses their trademark air of intellectual and moral superiority in any conflict with the mainstream, we have gained ground in the short term. But the longer-term goal will require patience. Because mainstream positions are based on historical experience and the accumulated wisdom of generations,[54] mainstream positions are more complex than liberal ones, and it takes longer for people to understand them.

As we have argued, political power is only the tip of the power iceberg. Political power rests on cultural and social power, and liberals dominate our culture from the White House to cocktail party conversations. So the principles and tools in the remainder of this book will apply to the cocktail party as much as to a televised debate between candidates. The principles will have to be adapted to the specific situations in which you find yourself.

Here are our new principles of engagement. The remainder of the book will cover practical tools and methods for living out each of these principles.

PRINCIPLES FOR MAINSTREAM ACTIVISTS

1. WE ARE THE MAINSTREAM AND LIBERALS ARE THE FRINGE. ACT LIKE IT.

Millions of mainstream Americans became more politically aware after the 2008 election and the blitzkrieg of leftist initiatives that followed. When speaking before groups of these new activists, a frequent comment that we heard was something like this:

> I was starting to wonder if I was out of touch. Everywhere I looked, Obama was being adored. It was only when I went to my first Tea Party rally that I realized I wasn't out of touch at all, that I wasn't the only one who thought that we as a country were heading in a dangerous direction.

Such is the power of the leftist institutions in controlling the political narrative that mainstream Americans can feel out of touch in our own country. Before anything else changes in this country, mainstream Americans will have to stop thinking like a helpless and out-of-touch minority and start thinking and acting like the big dogs on the political porch.

The most self-defeating habit of the mainstream is responding to hardcore leftist attacks by reasoning and defending our position. The mainstream must break forever the habit of defending mainstream beliefs to hardcore liberals, the habit of explaining ourselves and our beliefs to liberals as if common sense needed to be defended.

If the mainstream continues to waste time and energy defending that which should be accepted as given, then we are already defeated. We have to change that belief and begin acting like what we are: the mainstream majority in our country.

2. FACE YOUR FEAR OF DISAPPROVAL AND SOCIAL UNPLEASANTNESS.

The left uses the maturity and social decency of mainstream Americans as our Achilles' heel. If they call us the right names, if they ridicule us, if they question our integrity and intelligence, we will naïvely try to use evidence, reason, and facts to show them that they are wrong. In so doing, we give them the upper hand.

When we begin to use tactics that work, liberals will escalate. They will not surrender the schools, the news media, the churches, and the other cultural institutions willingly. They will get ugly, and then they will get uglier. We will need thick skins to save our republic. Our businesses might lose liberal customers. We might lose liberal friends. Liberal family members might shun us. After all, liberals might preach tolerance, but liberal hardliners rarely practice it. It is common for mainstream activists to receive harassing phone calls or even threats. Remember, the only known violence at a Tea Party event was when liberals beat up a vendor.

Yes, we will continue to be peaceful, law-abiding citizens. But we can no longer be the wusses of the political world who quiet down when liberals get loud and who defend ourselves against charges too absurd to warrant consideration.

3. NEVER, EVER FALL INTO A DEFENSIVE POSITION.

A major habit we have to break is letting the liberals use our maturity and social decency to put us on the defensive. When we try to disprove the baseless accusations of the left, we give them control of the political discussion. In so doing, we put ourselves in a weak and one-down position. This defensive posture has never been effective for combating the left's initiatives and attacks.

It is pointless to argue with leftists, but it is suicidal to compromise with them. The only effective strategy for dealing with the liberal threat will be to take power away from them—and keep it away.

4. SEIZE THE OFFENSIVE AND STAY ON IT.

The corollary to this last principle is that the mainstream has to seize the offensive and take control of the political narrative. Try to think back to the last major political initiative that was pushed by the mainstream. When was the last time the mainstream reduced the size and power of government and expanded the role of liberty?

If you answered "tax breaks," think again. Does getting to keep more of the money that was yours to begin with really constitute a political gain? If a thief takes your television but leaves your DVD player, have you really gained a DVD player? Tax breaks simply slow the expanse of government; they do not reverse it.

Now, when was the last time a federal department was reduced in size or eliminated completely? When was the last time a federal judge was impeached and removed from office for ignoring the clear meaning of the Constitution in favor of a leftist political agenda?

Instead of trying to stop whatever the liberals want to do to us next, we need to select the battlefield and show up first. We have to push our own plans for tax and education reform. We have to begin stripping leftist partisan groups from tax funding. We have to go after voter fraud with a vengeance. In short, we need to put the left on the political defensive and keep them there.

5. HIT HARD AND SUE FOR PEACE.

There is a subtle trap that awaits mainstream activists. Like the bully on the playground, liberals are prone to morph into victims in an instant if anyone calls them on their game.

When mainstream politicians do nothing more than point to the liberal record, liberals scream that the mainstreamer has "gone negative." Leftists know that this is just a tactic to keep the light of day away from their record, and conservatives know that too. But the danger is that this tactic might convince uninformed and misinformed voters that the mainstream is fighting dirty.

Our solution will be to respond to liberal attacks with a political hit so hard that the opponent's children will be born dizzy, and then to immediately seize the high moral ground by calling for an end to all the negativity.

Like we keep saying, this is politics, not civics.

6. DRIVE THE MAINSTREAM AGENDA THROUGH
THE CULTURE AND THE GOVERNMENT.

Because formal governmental power rests on cultural institutions, a return to legitimate constitutional government will mean a long mainstream march through the institutions currently held by the left. That might mean a brief conversation with strangers on an elevator, or it might mean changing what is taught in our schools.

Of course, given a choice between political action and mowing the lawn, most mainstreamers will choose mowing the lawn. We might get politically active when desperate, as millions of mainstreamers have since the election of Obama. But the moment we see some relief, our history suggests that we will want to go back to minding our own business.

That is precisely what the left is planning on. As many early patriots said, the price of liberty is eternal vigilance. They didn't say "occasional" vigilance. Citizens who are not politically savvy will eventually become subjects.

We have to learn to see every aspect of life, from our seat at the dinner table to seats in Congress and everything in between, as ground to be taken or lost in the struggle against liberalism.

From this day forward, *everything* is political.

7. INOCULATE CHILDREN AGAINST LIBERALISM.

Taking back the institutions will be a long struggle. Meanwhile, as we struggle, the left will continue teaching our children that their parents are backward and out of touch with new ways of thinking. They will continue to teach our children that America deserves the punishment that the liberals are meting out—indeed, that the Islamic terrorists and other enemies of America are meting out. They will continue working to subvert and turn our next generation into yet more liberals who will be de facto enlisted in the fight to drag America down into socialist tyranny.

So we have to inoculate the next generation against the left. There are excellent resources for doing this. There are excellent books that tell the real history of America. There are excellent books that tell the truth about the "climate change" scam. There are excellent websites and videos with plenty of information that can be used to combat liberalism. What the mainstream has to do is to get organized and use those resources.

The ideal first step is homeschooling to break the grip of the teachers' unions on the minds of our children, but we realize that many Americans will not take this step, especially with the likelihood of an Obama Depression looming over the next decade. So we will offer some ideas on what we call "guerilla education," the practice of teaching children the truth even when the government-run schools are attempting to indoctrinate them with falsehoods.

The fact that such an approach is even necessary is in itself evidence of how far the republic has fallen over the last century.

7

THINKING LIKE CITIZENS

The biggest barrier to restoration of the republic at this point is the attitude of helplessness in the minds of mainstream Americans, the attitude that arrogant and corrupt government is just a fact of life. We have forgotten that politicians get elected to be our employees, not our rulers.

Consider a common mainstream concern that vouchers would open the door to the federal government controlling the curriculum in private schools. Note the *assumption* that it would be up to the government to make the decision about the limits of the government's power over private education, and that the people paying for the system would have no say in how that system would run.

Through decades of the Long March, we have learned to ask, "What will the government let us do?" instead of, "What will we delegate to the government and what do we reserve for ourselves?" That is the way subjects think.

A citizen's attitude, one appropriate to life in a republic, is that the mainstream would tell the government that we are going to have a voucher system, and we would tell the government to keep its nose out of private schools. No debate. No discussion. Citizens don't give government the *option* to make decisions about private schools; subjects do that.

The first step back toward a healthy nation will be to change the self-defeating mindset of mainstream Americans. The mainstream has to stop thinking like subjects of a government; we need to start thinking like citizens of a republic.

PRINCIPLE 1: WE ARE THE MAINSTREAM AND LIB-ERALS ARE THE FRINGE. ACT LIKE IT.

We in the mainstream have lost so much of our freedom and tolerated such abuses of power, even when we win elections, that we have adopted a helpless mentality. It's as if mainstream taxpayers have learned to think like the subjects in psychological experiments on learned helplessness.[55] With prolonged exposure to conditions in which nothing they do affects their outcomes, humans and animals often fall into a passive, helpless posture. They give up. And even when the conditions are changed so that their actions could make a difference, subjects in these experiments have a hard time learning that their actions *do* make a difference.

Now think about the experience of the political mainstream. The left sets the agenda, and we react. They decide to go after our freedom of speech, and we pull out a First Amendment that means nothing to them. They decide to take over private companies, and we try to convince them not to, or at least not to spend more than they have to. When liberals call us nasty names, we somehow think that we have to *prove* to them that their charges are false. But nothing we do seems to make a difference.

Nothing we do makes a difference because we are constantly in a defensive posture. So the first big challenge for the mainstream is to accept the fact that we have learned to think like outsiders in our own country, like subjects whose wishes the government can ignore at will.

SEEING OUR POWER

As we have said, a prime rule in politics is that a small number of people with an agenda will dominate a larger number of people who just want to be left alone. The left has made effective use of that principle.

But what if mainstream Americans used the same principle? What if, for the first time in a century, the left had a *real* struggle on its hands? What if the left faced not just resistance from the mainstream but a positive mainstream agenda that took back the ground we had lost?

The 40 percent of the electorate who describe themselves as conservative are already with us. But when we reach the uninformed and misinformed, when we expose the real liberal agenda and character to them, many of them will break our way. They already do break our way at times, but we need to bring about a permanent shift in thinking that drives liberal ideas to the very fringes of society. Remember, the true heart of American liberalism cannot stand the light of day, so we need to shine the light on it.

And there are far more of us in the mainstream than there are on the left. We need only to start acting like a confident majority, from the water cooler at the office to news interviews to the halls of Congress.

"WE HOLD THESE TRUTHS TO BE SELF-EVIDENT . . ."

The Judeo-Christian worldview of our Founding Fathers led them to *assume* self-evident truths in the Declaration of Independence. Edmund Burke and later conservative writers explained that the conservative worldview derives in part from presumptions in favor of traditions that have stood the test of time. That is, the accumulated experience and wisdom of countless generations is passed on to us as traditions and things that we *assume to be true*. If some politician comes along promising to radically transform society, the conservative mind assumes it to be self-evident that such transformation would make things worse.[56]

What happened to this idea that "we hold these truths to be self-evident"? Liberals have taken skepticism to such an extreme that it has left them completely unmoored from any sense of self-evident truths.

There are no fixed reference points for the left other than their passing whims and preferences. One easily imagines college sophomores, having feasted on a steady diet of liberal skepticism, intoning the inevitable: "But how can we really know *anything?*"

It took centuries and the experience of millions of people in Western civilization to develop the cultural presumptions in favor of liberty that are captured in America's founding documents. It takes a liberal no time to challenge all of that with something like, "Government can buy medicine more cheaply than private citizens, so why shouldn't government just provide our medicine?"

Until the left seized control of our cultural institutions, the answer to such a question would have been, "It's obvious why government should not provide our medicine." No debate. No struggling to prove that liberty is better than governmental control. Just a built-in cultural assumption that it is self-evident that a government that provides your medicine can control your life.

Mainstream America needs to get back to the belief that there are some ideas about people and government that are just self-evident. What are some of these self-evident truths, the ones that from now on we should just refuse to debate? Here are just a few:

- The Constitution means what it says. Period. Anyone who says it's a "living document" really means that the Constitution is getting in the way of their personal agenda.
- Any reasonably informed citizen can understand the fundamental points of the Constitution; a law degree is not required to understand the essentials of what government is and is not permitted to do.
- The First Amendment does not mean "We hereby declare war on any public mention of God or any reference to our Judeo-Christian heritage."
- Free enterprise is fairer and more efficient and produces a higher standard of living than a government-controlled economy ever will. The worldwide evidence is so overwhelming that this case should be considered closed.

- If someone claims to be "intimidated" by perfectly reasonable protections against voter fraud, then they're planning to commit voter fraud.
- Unless there is substantial agreement among the mainstream about limits on liberty, liberty wins.

Why is this fundamental change in our thinking so critical? Let's offer an absurd example to make the point. Imagine being at a dinner party and some leftist says, "Professional football is too brutal and I think the federal government should outlaw it." Now, you could pull out the Constitution and ask where the government would get that authority. Or you could argue that the professionals know the risk of injury and voluntarily take that risk in order to reap the potential rewards.

But if you responded with these or any other reasonable points, you would have allowed the liberal to start a discussion about something that should not even be on the table. You would have given one liberal's whim the same weight as the accumulated wisdom that resulted in the limited role of government laid out in our founding documents. Even if your rebuttal is outstanding, you will have lost ground because you have allowed the liberal to make you defend that which should be obvious.

On the other hand, you could simply respond, "Wow. That's kinda out there, isn't it? Hey, who saw the game yesterday?"

That response says, in essence, "We hold it to be *self-evident* that the federal government has no say in this issue." The mainstream person should respond with the same attitude that he would use if the liberal had said that the federal government should regulate the pay of professional athletes or corporate executives, or that government should do something about incandescent light bulbs or health care.

YOU CAN BE A GOOD CITIZEN AND STILL HIT HARD

When we cover examples like the one above and describe other harder-hitting techniques to mainstream audiences, people sometimes say,

"But that seems so demeaning. I don't like to be that way. Isn't there another way?" If there were, mainstream America wouldn't be in the mess we're in today, because we've tried every other way of dealing with the left, and they have all failed.

It might help to remember that Christian football players can hit hard and still be Christians. Their religious commitment forbids them to hate their opponents or to purposefully injure them, but nothing in Christianity says that Christian athletes cannot play football and make a hard block or tackle. In the same way, nothing in Christianity forbids a Christian from fighting in a war to protect home and hearth. Nothing in Christianity says that Christians cannot use firearms to protect their families against intruders who threaten them. Christians do not join the military *in order* to kill, and no Christian would *hope* for an opportunity to use a firearm against another human being. And yes, we are commanded to love our enemies, but we can love liberals without allowing them to destroy the freest and most prosperous nation in history.

The same principle applies to using the tools of politics in the political struggle. Politics is about power and control and deciding who gets their way. Think of politics as an ideological contact sport. If we win, liberals will live along with us in a free and prosperous country. If liberals win, the light goes out in that shining city set upon a hill, as President Reagan described a free America.

If the thought of deliberately taking the wind out of a liberal's sails seems unkind or unfair to you, then you are experiencing the very niceness that liberals have used against us to dominate the mainstream. Good citizenship is more than working hard, paying taxes, and voting. It also means defending our society against its enemies. If you cannot get your mind around the necessity of demoralizing the enemy, you cannot win.

It's one thing to understand intellectually that you're doing the right thing when you embarrass liberals by exposing their hypocrisy, but it's another thing indeed to deal with the churning in your stomach when they look at you with hate in their eyes and start calling you names.

PRINCIPLE 2: FACE YOUR FEAR OF DISAPPROVAL AND SOCIAL UNPLEASANTNESS.

There is an insight that can be very liberating when dealing with other people in general, and most especially with angry, critical liberals: Other people would be basically the way they are if they had never met you. That does not mean that your behavior is unimportant, and, of course, it does not give you license to do whatever you wish. But it does imply that, if liberals are offended by a mainstream value that you have expressed, or if they call you names or get angry, they would be offended by something and angrily calling someone names even if they had never met you. *It has nothing to do with you.* That's just what liberals do. And they do it predictably in a wide range of situations. If you tiptoe around liberals in an effort to avoid their displeasure, you will spend your life on your tiptoes and liberals will still be mad at somebody about something.

Remember that the source of your discomfort in those situations is your childhood conscience, the early messages that tell us to be nice and not to cause unpleasantness. But the childhood conscience is just there to help us get along until we develop an adult conscience. You might feel uncomfortable at the sight of the liberal's anger, especially when that anger is focused on you. At such times, just remember that the source of liberal anger, hatred, and misery is inside of them. The source of their dyspeptic character is their moral nihilism and a lust for power that can never be satisfied. There is no bottom to the hole of nihilism, and no human being can successfully make the world conform to their wishes. You are not the cause of liberal anger; you are just a witness to it.

When we learn to better stand our ground in the face of liberal pressure, the mainstream will have to get through some very uncomfortable moments. Fortunately, athletes and other performers have learned many techniques over the years for managing the stress of performing in public. Some of these tools will be helpful for Good Citizens who step into the madcap world of politics.

To understand these tools, we need to take a very brief look at why our brains seem to shut down sometimes when we are under stress, such as when we are dealing with liberals.

ANATOMY OF THE APPEASEMENT CYCLE

A quick look at some basic brain functioning will help to explain why our minds sometimes go blank under stress and what we can do to keep them sharp and focused.[57]

When we are thinking rationally, like when considering the impact of high taxes on job creation, our brains show increased activity in an area in the front called the cortex. This portion of the brain is sometimes called the "executive" portion, in that it is involved in reasoning, planning, and decision-making. When this area of the brain is fully engaged, our private experience is one of being clear-headed and focused.

When we encounter a potential threat, however, such as hearing a deep growl coming from a bush behind us, there is a surge of activity in structures deeper in the brain called the limbic system. The limbic system triggers the release of adrenalin and other chemicals to prepare us to escape or to confront the threat. That's why we feel our hearts racing, our muscles tensing, and other powerful physical changes.

We know what these survival responses feel like if we are facing a threat to our physical well-being. But the same portions of the brain respond to social threats. For an athlete or a musician performing in front of a large audience, the threat can be something as simple as making a mistake and being embarrassed, or suffering the disapproval of others. Add a heckler in the bleachers behind a batter, or a music critic sitting in the front row in front of a musician, and the degree of social threat is increased even more. Any situation in which we are being judged or evaluated can trigger these survival responses—we experience them as anxiety, nervousness, or the jitters—as any student taking an exam knows.

Depending on your role, you will encounter plenty of difficult social situations as you become more engaged in political activity. Speaking in public settings like Tea Party rallies, addressing your grievances to elected bodies, participating in interviews with hostile reporters, becoming a candidate and having to debate a leftist opponent—all of these situations may trigger these uncomfortable emotions.

But when you need to keep a clear head, these emotional responses are more than just uncomfortable; they can really interfere with your focus and mental clarity. The emergency functions of the limbic system are wired to take over when we encounter a threat, even a social threat. When the emotional limbic system shows increased activity, we see decreased activity in the executive areas needed for reasoning. That is why we don't think as clearly when we are emotional, as we might be while debating a liberal or addressing a liberal school board.

The tendency of the deeper limbic system to take over your brain under stress is critical if you are running from a tiger, when being fast is more important than being smart. But it also explains why you forget your points in the heat of a debate, and then you remember everything you should have said after the debate is over and your brain has returned to normal. To make things worse for the new political activist, research shows that even relatively small surges in the defensive centers of our brain are enough to limit our ability to think clearly.

These stress responses also help to explain why we get drawn into debating bizarre claims by liberals, and, even worse, why we sometimes give in and appease them. When we are under stress, we fall back on well-learned habits. The habits of explaining, clarifying, and even compromising have worked for years when dealing with other mainstream Americans who share our values. But we may also fall back on those when we are dealing with the leftists, the political equivalent of hecklers in our national bleachers.

The left has learned to exploit mainstream people's natural tendency to go into defensive mode in the face of a threat. Look at the familiar pattern that we see in political exchanges between mainstream candidates and leftists. Often mainstream candidates seem to be caught off guard by a "gotcha" question from the media, or by some bizarre accusation from a leftist candidate. All too often, mainstream candidates fall into the trap of trying to convince the leftist that they do not hate poor people, that they want children to learn to read, that they really are not out to destroy the planet, and so on.

All too often, mainstream people fall back on appeasement as an effort to escape the unpleasantness.

Let's look at some simple tools to help you stay focused when you face the liberal hecklers.

CALM THE BODY TO CLEAR THE MIND

When we are anxious before some big event, well-intentioned friends will offer advice like, "What's the worst that can happen? Come on, you're making too much out of this."

The problem is that their advice is aimed at the executive brain, which, during a confrontation, steps into the backseat so that the limbic system can drive. Instead of thinking clearly in order to calm down, the trick is to calm down so you can think clearly.

A common physical response to a stressful event is to start breathing in a shallow manner. Think about a recent experience in which you were startled. You might have actually "caught your breath" for an instant, the most extreme version of shallow breathing. A second common physical response to a stressful event is to tighten your muscles in preparation for the fight-or-flight response. You might experience this tightness as jitters or nervousness. When you are experiencing these physical sensations, the limbic system is running the show.

RELEASE THE PHYSICAL TENSION

The first technique to learn is how to take the physical energy out of the emotional surge. To do that, simply breathe deeply and relax your body as soon as you begin to experience the physical sensations of stress. If that sounds too simple, remember that this method has been shown to manage stress for decades across a wide range of performance situations. The problem isn't whether the method works; the problem is remembering to use it when you most need it.

The earlier you spot the change in your breathing and the tension in your body, the sooner you can head off the emotional surge. The specific pattern varies somewhat from person to person. For some, the first cue that we are getting into defensive mode is "butterflies" in the stomach. For others, the shoulders tense up. Still others may feel their heart pounding. By learning where you experience emotional stress in your body, you can learn to focus your attention on those areas and purposefully relax those muscles.

Breathe and relax; it's that simple. But it's not just any breath that works. It's best to take a deep, slow breath from your diaphragm (around your belt area) and gently release the air. This breath should be noticeably slower and deeper than a normal breath, maybe six or seven seconds of inhaling before you release the air. Pull the air as far down toward your belt as you can before you let your upper chest expand. Then, as you release the air, deliberately let your muscles relax so that they feel like they are sagging. For many people, the muscles in the neck, shoulders, and back are especially important to relax.

Some people find it helpful to imagine that they are breathing air into those areas of tension, visualize that breath gathering up or absorbing the tension like a sponge absorbing water, and then breathing out that tension as if squeezing the water out of a sponge. If that helps you, do it. If not, just concentrate on calming your breathing and releasing muscle tension. You should learn to do this in such a way that no one even notices you doing it.

This simple method has worked for years with athletes, actors, musicians, and others who have to calm their nerves in order to perform at their best. It's important to practice this skill when the stakes are relatively low so that you will be able to do it well when you are in the heat of the political struggle. So practice it when you are in a traffic jam, in an action movie where you feel yourself tensing up during the intense scenes, in line at the grocery store, and other situations that are relatively benign. The better you get at doing this, the more you will be able to drain the energy out of the fear that is the liberal's secret weapon.

It may take a few seconds, but as the blood flows from the limbic system back to the reasoning centers of the brain, you will be able to think much more clearly. In later chapters, we will give you powerful tools to seize the initiative against a liberal in that moment.

UNDERSTAND THE THREAT

For many people, simply taking the energy out of the stress response is enough for them to clear their minds and perform better. Others find that they need to understand the source of the emotional discomfort. They want to understand why they would respond to something as simple as a heated discussion or an interview with a reporter with the same emotions that are designed to protect them from a life-threatening situation.

It is helpful to realize that these visceral emotional responses are often vestiges of the childhood conscience. In childhood, we often experienced anger and disappointment from others when we did something that violated the rules. These feeling-habits can continue even as we develop a more mature sense of morality, and sometimes those feelings lurk just underneath.

For instance, if someone in authority questioned our actions or motives, we felt the need to explain ourselves. And liberals almost always present themselves as authorities—on economics, morality, science, history, you name it, they're smarter and better than the rest of us. The temptation to explain yourself in the face of liberal pontificating is likely nothing more than these old habits.

The point is to remember that liberal hostility and name-calling do not mean that you have done something wrong; they mean that liberals are angry because they are not getting their way.

PRINCIPLE 3: NEVER, EVER FALL INTO A DEFENSIVE POSITION.

Mainstream Americans fall into the defensive trap for several reasons. First, we explain and defend because those are deeply ingrained habits. Due to the messages in our childhood conscience, we feel uncomfortable when others think badly of us. When leftists make some horrible accusation against us, we simply fall into the old habit of trying to explain ourselves.

Second, we take liberals at their word. We have trouble believing that someone would make an accusation that they know to be false, such as claiming that it is racist to want to control your own health care or that conservative talk shows cause mass shootings.

Because the accusations are so irrational, we believe that we can disprove them with evidence and reason. After all, evidence and reason pay off when dealing with others in the mainstream. But with liberals, the truthfulness of the accusation is irrelevant; they are only concerned with its impact. The real action is going on beneath the surface of the spoken words.

Finally, when we feel attacked, our brains shift into defensive mode in order to prepare us for a flight-or-fight response. The problem is that we don't think as clearly, so we fall back on habitual responses such as explaining and defending. Slowing the pace with a deep breath, even for a couple of seconds, can give you valuable time to check that habitual response and choose a more effective one.

TWO LEVELS OF DISCUSSION

Much human communication, including political communication, happens below the level of the actual words that are spoken. And much of that nonverbal communication happens without us being very aware of it. We pick up on all kinds of subtle cues that tell us quite a bit about what's going on underneath the spoken words.

That's why e-mail messages can be so easily misinterpreted; we are missing the subtle nonverbal cues that tell us how to interpret what is being said.

Have you ever been channel surfing and paused for a moment on a channel in a language that you don't speak? It's amazing how much you can pick up on even when you have no idea what the words mean. You can tell if the conversation is light or serious. You can tell if there is trust or tension between the people talking. And you can tell if one of the people has more *power* than the others. You can easily tell if one party is confronting and the other is defending by the underlying tone of the conversation. We call that underlying tone the "unspoken narrative." It's the nonverbal story beneath the spoken story.

Even when you don't speak the language, your brain still picks up on countless cues about what is going on. Of course, the same happens when you *do* speak the language.

Imagine a young man at a health club working out on a machine near an attractive young lady, and imagine that he strikes up a conversation with, "Do you come in here often?" If you overheard him, you would not think that he was conducting marketing research for the health club. You would know without a doubt that he was saying, in essence, "You're cute and I'd like to get to know you." Likewise, you would interpret her polite but cool "No" as saying, "Forget it. You're not my type." On the other hand, "I've just joined. How about you?" could mean, "You're kind of cute. It's OK to talk to me."

We learn to read these subtle social cues without thinking about them, just as we learn the rules of our culture, and they are just as powerful in shaping our behavior. Have you ever observed that someone you know seems to "walk on eggshells" around someone else? Or have you met someone who just seemed to radiate "I'm too important to be here" at a social event? It would be hard to put into words exactly how we pick up on these cues, but we recognize them without thinking much about it. And those subtle cues can have a profound effect on how we behave and how others perceive us.

And when it comes to much of our political discourse, these subtle cues convey a sense of intellectual and moral superiority on the left and a sense of uncertainty and defensiveness among the mainstream.

THE UNSPOKEN NARRATIVE IN AMERICAN POLITICS

Watch liberal politicians on television and try to ignore the actual topic, focusing instead on the underlying tone of the discussion. What attitude seems to seep from a liberal's pores, regardless of the words that they say? With liberals, you will often detect an underlying tone of intellectual and moral superiority. And often, there is also a subtle hint of, "I am willing to get pretty unpleasant if you cross me." You've learned to pick up on these cues from your earliest experiences with difficult people, but you might not really have paid attention to those patterns in politics.

Now watch mainstream politicians and citizens in encounters with liberals. Regardless of the spoken words, who seems to have the upper hand? Usually it is the leftist who is on the offensive. Which one stops talking when the other one interrupts? Usually the mainstream politician submits to being interrupted. Who seems to be dominant and confident, and who seems to be on the defensive and trying too hard to explain themselves? All too often, the mainstreamers come across, at the level of the unspoken narrative, like youngsters trying to explain themselves to a scolding teacher.

Regardless of the actual topic of discussion, the underlying pattern is almost always the same: The liberals are on the offensive, and the rest of us on are the defensive. To really get a sense of how the left bullies the mainstream, try a simple experiment. For the next week, pay attention to those subtle cues when you watch coverage of politicians in the news. Try to ignore the actual content of what they're saying and focus just on the underlying dynamics. Who accuses and who defends? Who interrupts? Who sets the terms of the discussion?

Unless the conservative is Ann Coulter, you will likely have a sickening realization of just how badly liberals dominate both the unspoken and the spoken narrative, and just how meekly most mainstream Americans accept it. When confronted with some bizarre statement from the left, it is as if mainstream Americans say, "Wait a minute. Let me think. I think I've got a good answer for that one." In the underlying narrative, the one beneath the spoken words, the liberal has really said, "I can make you dance to my tune" and the mainstreamer has said, "Oh, but just watch how well I can dance."

Consider as an example the underlying message in all of the demands of politically correct speech. "Black" is out, "African American" is in. "Illegal alien" is out, "undocumented worker" is in. Nobody says "global warming" anymore. Now we all have to say "climate change." The actual *topic* of politically correct speech is irrelevant. The underlying narrative is simple: "Liberals can control the very language you use. Get used to it."

DEFENDING MAKES THE INCREDIBLE CREDIBLE

Our tendency to defend actually helps the left in their Long March. When we defend against absurd charges—say, that taxpayers in the Tea Party are dangerous extremists—we actually give credibility to the charge. It is as if we are saying that the charge *merits* a response. When a mainstreamer starts out a statement by saying, "I don't have anything against Mexicans, but I'm concerned about the impact of illegal immigration," he has actually accepted the absurd premise that wanting an orderly process for entering this country is somehow morally suspect.

When we defend against liberal accusations one-on-one or in small group settings, we have allowed liberals to control the topic and boost their sense of power. But when that happens in enough settings over a long enough time, we have allowed the left to control the narrative of our entire national discourse. The uninformed will passively absorb the left's subtle premises, and the misinformed will be even more misinformed.

So once we start thinking that we have to defend mainstream beliefs, we have already lost control of the narrative at both the spoken and the unspoken levels. Liberals have defined the charges against us, and we have spent our time defending ourselves instead of pushing our own agenda.

THE "FILLING IN THE BLANKS" TECHNIQUE

Because the tendency to defend in the face of liberal attacks can be so natural and so automatic, we recommend that you use a technique called "filling in the blanks" as a means of quickly diagnosing the attack and taking care not to fall into a defensive position.

First, translate the liberal's attack, accusation, or demand into the following format:

LIBERAL: *"You are bad because you [fill in the blank]."*

Regardless of the surface topic—racism, taxes, sexism, health care, homeland security—leftists are almost always saying, in essence, "You are bad because you [fill in the blank]."

And notice the strong tendency for mainstream Americans to respond with something like this:

MAINSTREAMER: *"You've misunderstood me. I was just trying to [fill in the blank]."*

If we go that route, we've already lost because we have allowed the left to decide the terms of the discussion:

LIBERAL: *"Let's do this. I'll make accusations and you defend yourself, and nothing you say will change my mind. Have we got a deal?"*

When we bring it to the surface, no one would have a discussion on those terms. But watch mainstream politicians in debates and news interviews and see how often they fall into that precise pattern. Or notice how often *you* fall into it when you're talking with leftists. When mainstreamers defend ourselves with reason and evidence against liberal demands and accusations, we are doing something far worse than just wasting our time. We are surrendering to the underlying pattern of liberal dominance and mainstream appeasement. Every time a liberal puts a mainstreamer on the defensive, liberal confidence is boosted and that of the mainstream is drained.

You Four-Eyed Racist!

Before we move on to methods for seizing the offensive, we want to hammer home the importance of staying out of the defensive trap. We also want to hammer home the point that the spoken narrative in liberal attacks may change but the underlying narrative is always the same. Until mainstream activists recognize this, we will be in the trap before we know it.

Let's start with an absurd example before we move to a more serious one. We know that the liberal tactic of name-calling is not driven by a rational appraisal of our character; instead, it is the intellectual equivalent of calling us "Four Eyes" if we happen to wear glasses. Most of us wouldn't even think of trying to use reason in the face of such an absurd accusation. But if we did, the underlying pattern of liberal attacks and mainstream defense would look like this:

LIBERAL: *"Four Eyes!"*

MAINSTREAMER: *"Oh, my goodness! You've misunderstood me, and I think I can clear things up for you. My glasses may look to you like an extra pair of eyes; but, you see, they really aren't eyes, they're corrective lenses."*

LIBERAL: *"Four Eyes! You've got four eyes!"*

MAINSTREAMER: *"No, really, I don't have four eyes. See, I wear glasses to help me see better, but the glasses are not really eyes. Look, I can take them off. See? I have two eyes, just like you. You know, we're really not all that different."*

LIBERAL: *"You're a four-eyed freak, that's what you are! You're a mutant!"*

MAINSTREAMER: *"OK, OK! I'll put in my contacts."*

Crude as that example may be, you will see the same underlying pattern in every news interview and every political debate between leftists and mainstreamers, regardless of the issue being debated. In essence, the mainstreamer allows the liberal to define the topic as "Prove that you're not a mutated freak of nature with four eyes." The mainstreamer is on the defensive from the moment the liberal's premise becomes accepted as the topic for discussion.

Now for a more realistic example. Though the surface discussion may sound more sensible than the "Four Eyes" example, notice how this typical discussion about illegal immigration follows the same underlying pattern of liberal attack and mainstream defense. The unspoken narrative is exactly the same.

LIBERAL: *"We need amnesty for undocumented workers. It's the only fair thing."*

MAINSTREAMER: *"But I'm concerned that they've broken our laws, and we would set a dangerous precedent by ignoring that. Don't you see the danger of telling people it's OK to ignore the law? I mean, what if everyone decided to stop obeying traffic signs—"*

LIBERAL: *"Oh, I see. You hate Mexicans, don't you?"*

MAINSTREAMER: *"What? You've misunderstood me. I like Mexicans just fine. In fact, I speak a little Spanish. I have friends who are Latino. I'm just trying to make sure that people who come into this country—"*

LIBERAL: *"It's the skin color isn't it? All this opposition to amnesty is nothing but a cover for your stone-cold racism."*

MAINSTREAMER: *"That's not true. Why, just last week we had a cookout and invited our good friends José and Rosita. And I support legal immigration. I just want immigrants in this country to follow our laws. In fact, our laws are much more lenient that the immigration laws in Mexico."*

LIBERAL: *"But Mexico isn't a mean country like this one. And Mexico isn't filled with racists like so many people in America."*

MAINSTREAMER: *"Well, I suppose a limited amnesty might work, just to handle the current situation. But I wouldn't want it to become a pattern."*

LIBERAL: *"Yeah, limited amnesty. That's the idea. Just this one time. Yeah. Oh, by the way, once we have limited amnesty, we need to let them vote. It's only fair."*

Look back over the above exchange. What is the surface narrative, the spoken one? Quite clearly, the liberal has defined the narrative as "Anyone who opposes amnesty is racist."

But notice that the underlying narrative hasn't changed. It doesn't matter whether the liberal is calling us "Four Eyes" or "racist." That pattern is the same. Who is on the offensive, calling the shots? Who is on the defensive, trying to get out of an uncomfortable corner? The leftist defines the topic to be discussed and stays on the attack; the mainstreamer attempts to reason, to no avail.

That has been the pattern behind the Long March. If reasoning with liberals hasn't worked in the last hundred years, why would mainstream Americans think it would start working now?

It's worth a reminder here that, in an innocent effort to correct the obvious non sequitur that opposition to amnesty is racist, the mainstreamer has inadvertently given that premise legitimacy. The defense has made the incredible credible. If someone calls you "Four Eyes" and you try to explain that your glasses are not eyes, you have accepted their premise as a legitimate starting point for discussion. Likewise, if you try to prove to a leftist hardliner that it is not racist to oppose amnesty, you have accepted that premise as worthy of discussion.

This method has allowed the radical left to seize what appears to be the moral high ground in every debate. Their position is: If you don't want the bureaucrats and despots at the United Nations to dictate our environmental policy, you must not care about the environment. If you don't want some government union member making decisions about your health care, you must want children to go without medical care. The irony of moral nihilists seizing the moral high ground stuns the senses.

What a Difference a Backbone Makes

So what do we do instead? To give you a preview of the methods we are about to cover, let's play these examples out again. This time, let's put a little backbone in the mainstreamer. First, let's look at a different pattern in the case of the glasses:

LIBERAL: *"Four Eyes!"*

MAINSTREAMER: *"Hey everybody, Chuckles here can't tell the difference between glasses and eyes."*

Notice the subtle difference? OK, so it's not subtle, but it's not meant to be. Instead of accepting the absurd accusation as even worthy of discussion, the mainstreamer offers a new premise that the liberal is clownish and hopelessly out of it. The liberal's verbal offensive has been stopped in its tracks. The underlying narrative has changed from "mainstream on the defensive" to "the liberal is kooky."

Of course, we are not suggesting that you stoop to calling liberals names. In fact, you will only sink to the left's level if you do. So the actual words you use will be more appropriate than in our example above, but the unspoken narrative of your response should convey: "Nice try, but we're not going to play that."

Now let's replay the illegal immigration example and show what a difference a little backbone can make. This time, the spoken words of the mainstreamer would be perfectly appropriate for a political debate, but the underlying tone would still send the leftist a clear message that this discussion will not follow the old script. Note how the mainstreamer changes both the unspoken narrative and the spoken one.

LIBERAL: *"All this opposition to amnesty is nothing but a cover for stone-cold racism."*

MAINSTREAMER: *"So you're defending massive voter fraud?"*

LIBERAL: *"Nobody said anything about voter fraud. I just want amnesty for people—"*

MAINSTREAMER: *"Come on, now. You know exactly what amnesty is all about, and so does everyone else. It's a tool to get illegal aliens registered to vote. Liberal policies have alienated the American mainstream, so voter fraud using illegal aliens is the only way to make up for those losses."*

LIBERAL: *"You're just saying that because they're Mexicans and their skin—"*

MAINSTREAMER: *"Have you ever really thought about what voter fraud does? It robs law-abiding citizens of their votes. Robs them! How fair is that? How can anyone defend canceling out the votes of law-abiding, taxpaying citizens?*

LIBERAL: *"Four Eyes!"*

The unspoken narrative of liberal moral superiority would have been broken as long as the mainstreamer counterattacked instead of defending. But this specific counterattack changes the narrative of the debate from "opposing amnesty is racist" to "amnesty is a cover for voter fraud." The mainstreamer has seized the offensive, and the liberal must go on defense.

And the last part was only half-joking. If you refuse to let a hardcore leftist define the narrative and you hold your ground, expect to be called names.

By the way, note the power in the above example of asking questions. Other than times when we are asking a favor or asking for directions, the act of questioning often sets up a subtle power difference. Remember the old "Where have you been?" tone from childhood? Or being called upon to answer a question by a teacher? If you do it right, just the act of asking the leftist a good question starts to send a message that you are not on the defensive. When you are debating a leftist and need a moment to think, a good technique is simply to ask them a question.

So watch for the left's intended narrative, the debate they want to have, and refuse to debate on their terms. Then seize control of the narrative and make them debate on *your* terms.

The method is not hard to use, and it is easy to remember. The hard part is breaking the habit of trying to defend yourself against charges that you know are absurd.

You will not convince the hardcore leftist, by the way, but then you are not trying to. Your intended audience is uninformed and misinformed voters who have to choose between "racism" and "voter fraud" as explanations for opposition to amnesty. By keeping the liberal on the defensive, you have set up a subtle sense that the liberals are trying to hide something. (They are.)

THE TINFOIL HAT RULE

As a memory aid, we suggest that all mainstreamers learn and practice the Tinfoil Hat Rule when tempted to reason with the unreasonable:

> Never allow someone wearing a tinfoil hat to control the narrative, and never allow someone who *should* be wearing a tinfoil hat to control the narrative.

If you allow someone in a tinfoil hat to control the conversation at a dinner party, you will have to listen to a lot of stuff about messages from outer space. If you allow left-wing hardliners to control the narrative on the national scene, you will have to listen to a lot of stuff about how the solution to our debt crisis is to borrow and spend more money, or how American success is responsible for poverty in other countries.

Of course, tinfoil hats are a state of mind; an actual tinfoil hat is not required.

Once the mainstream starts thinking like citizens instead of subjects, we will be ready to start *acting* like citizens instead of subjects.

8

ACTING LIKE CITIZENS

PRINCIPLE 4: SEIZE THE OFFENSIVE
AND STAY ON IT.

The following methods can be used in one-on-one encounters with liberals, in informal settings with groups of people, and in formal debates and campaign statements. When mainstream thinking dominates the culture—as it should—there will be very few places in America where leftist dogma can put down roots.

You will, of course, have to adapt these methods to fit the particular situation. But remember, the goals of all of the methods are to isolate the left, to dominate the political narrative, and to educate the uninformed and misinformed.

BE CLEAR ABOUT YOUR GOALS

Regardless of the setting in which you use these methods, one goal will always be to take the wind out of the hardcore left's sails. A defining characteristic of the hardcore left is the smug attitude of intellectual and moral superiority. When they use their tactics, such as attacking the person instead of debating an issue, they are accustomed to walking away with an attitude that says, "I guess I told *them* a thing or two!" One purpose of the following methods is to deprive them of that sense of success, so that liberals leave encounters with the mainstream thinking something like, "Whoa, that didn't work out like I planned."

Put another way, we want the schoolyard bully to start thinking, "Uh-oh. Nobody looks scared of me anymore. I'd better keep a low profile."

ISOLATING AND DOMINATING THE LEFT

This goal is important even if you are engaging a liberal in a one-on-one encounter with no one else around. Each time their tactics backfire, liberals will become a little more demoralized politically, and every politically demoralized liberal represents one less threat to legitimate government.

If others are present, in situations ranging from a lively debate at a party all the way up to a formal political debate, you still want to isolate the hardcore leftist so that he comes across as out on the fringe of political thinking. And you want to maintain control of the political narrative—that is, the topic being discussed, the assumptions about that topic, and the meaning or interpretation that is given to that topic.

EDUCATING THE UNINFORMED

It is easier to reach uninformed voters who sometimes vote with the left and sometimes vote with the mainstream, so telling them apart from the hardcore leftists is important. This distinction will be most relevant in informal discussions with individuals and small groups. In more structured settings, such as a news interview or formal debates, you can just assume that some of those who will eventually be influenced by the results fall into the uninformed category.

Uninformed voters

- Share many values with the mainstream but are not especially interested in politics.
- Do not have a well-defined political philosophy.
- Like to keep political discussions short; they are more likely to shut down in a prolonged political discussion than to fall back on name-calling and spouting liberal talking points.
- Are probably cynical about both political parties.
- Are the true swing voters who vote based on their current personal situation, on the attractiveness of the candidates, and in keeping with the way that the prevailing political winds seem to be blowing.

With uninformed voters, it will often be enough to

- Highlight the nonsensical and hypocritical nature of leftist positions.
- Create the impression of a massive movement away from liberal candidates and policies (e.g., "I think most people are just trying to survive until the next election so we can get these radicals out of power and put the country back on a sane course").
- Point to the threats to their personal resources and freedom of choice that are represented by liberal positions.
- Highlight the unfairness of liberal actions.
- Emphasize that you are talking about sensible positions versus nonsensical positions, not Democrat versus Republican. If you try to defend Republicans who vote with the leftists, you will quickly lose credibility and get labeled as just another political hack.

EDUCATING THE MISINFORMED

Of course, often there will be no clear dividing line between the uninformed and the misinformed, but there are plenty of times in which the distinction can be useful. Like the uninformed, the misinformed will actually share many values with the mainstream. The misinformed are different from the uninformed in that the misinformed have more interest in politics and see themselves as well informed. The problem is that their sources of information have been the educational and news institutions controlled by the far left.

The misinformed differ from the hardcore leftists in that the misinformed will not knowingly take a position they know to be damaging to the country or unfair to others. Essentially, if misinformed liberals can realize that they have been wearing a tinfoil hat, they will want to take it off. The hardcore leftist will just insist that everyone else must start wearing tinfoil hats.

You will often find that misinformed people

- Pride themselves on being well informed but do not realize that the "information" they have been getting in school or on the news is heavily filtered and distorted.
- Are more likely than the uninformed to spout statistics or talking points that have come from leftist politicians and been blindly adopted by the liberal media. So the solution to Warren Buffet's secretary paying a higher tax rate than Warren Buffet will always be higher taxes on those the media label as "rich," not the Fair Tax or a flat tax, about which they have not heard.
- Are somewhat more likely than uninformed people to be seduced by the air of intellectual and moral superiority exuded by the left.
- Are unlikely, however, to come across as angry, hateful, or wanting America to be punished because of its past prosperity.
- Are more likely than uninformed people to have some of their ego tied up in being trendy and "with it," as defined by the educational system, news media, and entertainment media.

When misinformed voters convey an air of intellectual and moral superiority, more likely than not they have simply absorbed the assumptions of the liberal institutions. Their air of superiority will seem less desperate and toxic than that of the hardcore leftist; misinformed liberals do not have the same desperate need to dominate or manipulate others.

Because misinformed voters do pride themselves on being informed, a confrontational approach with them is likely to backfire. Remember, they don't hate America, and their liberal positions are not intended to be self-serving. The key is for them to see that sweet-sounding liberal policies actually hurt those they claim to help.

Some pointers when talking with misinformed voters:

- Remember that their rhetoric may sound liberal because they have been immersed in liberal dogma, but the *meaning* of their words is probably not that different from that of the mainstream. For example, misinformed voters who talk about racism are genuinely concerned about racism; they are not using the word to manipulate people, as does the hardcore left.
- Listen for and acknowledge possible areas of common ground. For example, if they parrot the left's position that "George Bush's policies started the economic mess," don't make excuses for Bush. They are right on that one, so agree up front and move on to common ground, that government spending is the cause of our economic mess, regardless of which party does the spending.
- Pace yourself. Whenever possible, as with a college student who comes home with some strange new ideas, genuine give-and-take over time will go a long way. Remember that they see themselves as well informed. If you hit them too hard or too fast with contradictory information, they are more likely to just shut you out in order to defend themselves. Point by point, example by example, give them time to come around. Often, these are the people who call Rush and say, "I used to hate you but then I started listening to you." They're the ones who thought they were liberal but who have been "Hannitized" after months of hearing Sean offering a perspective that is new to them.

- Ask questions to clarify their thinking so that you can spot the problems. What information do they have, and what are they missing? We are always surprised to find out how many misinformed liberal voters do not know that half of voters pay no federal income taxes. When they find that out, many can see the built-in conflict of interest when people can vote for more government without having to *pay* for more government.

- Listen for unspoken assumptions and draw those to the surface where the implications can be examined. In particular, what assumptions are they making about the role of government? If they talk about the rich paying "their fair share," ask them whether the purpose of taxation is to fund the government or to redistribute earnings; ask them who defines "rich"; bring up cases of entrepreneurs who only became rich after years of sacrifice and lower earnings; and so on. Where are there inconsistencies or implications that they haven't considered? For example, if they argue for socialized medicine on the grounds that the government can buy medicine in bulk cheaper than private citizens can, explore that line of thinking: The government can also buy food, housing, clothing, and firearms in bulk. So where does it stop? If the government can buy your medicine, what else can the government do? The point is to draw them away from the level of practical rhetoric where liberalism sounds so good (what can government do for you?) to the deeper level of basic principles where liberalism falls apart (what authority does government have, and where does it get that authority?).

- When pacing is not possible, as in a formal debate or campaign, it is important to discredit the left's positions without appearing to be negative. Remember, part of the leftist lie is that telling the truth about leftists is "negative campaigning." Later we will give you a method for hitting hard without coming across as negative.

Because misinformed voters share many values with the mainstream, the main strategy is to find those common values and expose liberal hypocrisy. Remember, anything that smells of "I told you so" will make it harder for them to admit that they are wrong. The non-verbal as well as the verbal exchange should respect their basic intentions and share their concerns wherever possible, because their basic worldview and their fundamental character are the same as those of the mainstream.

Now, let's move on to the central tool you will use.

HOW THE NARRATIVE GETS FRAMED

Think of the political narrative as a mental frame that we put around the political picture in front of us. That frame includes

- What we pay attention to.
- The assumptions that lie underneath our statements and positions.
- The meaning we give to what we see.

Let's look at an example. In dealing with his state's spending crisis in 2010, Governor Chris Christie of New Jersey inspired millions of mainstreamers when a teacher complained to Christie in front of a town hall meeting that she was underpaid, given her education and experience.[58]

Notice that we can use the filling in the blanks technique to expose the liberals' underlying message to the governor:

You are bad because you (don't pay teachers enough).

A typical mainstream response would run along these lines:

You've misunderstood me. I was just trying to (get the state out of its spending crisis).

Had he followed that path, Governor Christie would have been debating the issue on terms defined by the teachers' union. In fact, Christie almost took the bait when he pointed out to the teacher and the audience that the salary she stated did not include benefits:

CHRISTIE: *"You know what, you're getting paid more than that if you include . . . the cost of your benefits, the cost of your pension, and you include your paid holidays."*

He would have been right, of course, but then he would have made the classic mistake that mainstreamers make with liberals. The topic, the frame around the discussion, would still have been the issue of whether Christie's policies resulted in teachers being underpaid. How can anyone convince people who want more money that they are being paid enough?

But then Christie brilliantly recovered, and his handling of the situation was so masterful that it is worth using as an extended example of what we mean by "framing the narrative" and how to take control of the narrative away from the left.

FOCUSING ATTENTION: WHAT TOPIC ARE WE DISCUSSING?

When we focus attention on a particular topic, we are saying, in essence, "This is the topic that we are going to discuss." Framing a topic is like cropping a picture: We put some topics inside the frame and exclude others. Focusing attention is a major first step in putting a frame around any debate or discussion, in that it decides which topics are to be discussed and which are not.

The left has dominated the political narrative in this country because they choose which topics will be discussed and, all too often, the mainstream starts out on a losing path by allowing them to do so.

The teacher's challenge to Governor Christie focused attention on the adequacy of her pay as the issue to be discussed. The topic on the table was, in effect, "What are you going to do about the fact that I'm underpaid?" A typical mainstream politician would have walked right into the trap.

Governor Christie didn't. He didn't accept teacher pay as the topic on the table. Instead, he confidently reminded her that she didn't have to teach:

> CHRISTIE: *"Well you know what, then you don't have to do it . . . and teachers go into it knowing what the pay scale is."*

As we will discuss shortly, Governor Christie had just reframed the discussion from the issue of teachers' pay to one of personal responsibility for one's career choices. His next statement refocused the discussion from teacher pay onto the tactics of the union:

> CHRISTIE: *"What I'm saying is that in times of economic crisis this whole argument is over the fact that I asked people to not take a raise for a year and to pay 1.5 percent of their salary towards their benefits, and your union has said that that is the greatest assault on public education in the history of the state."*

By this simple statement, he moved the frame away from the topic the teacher wanted and on to aspects of the political picture that he wanted the public to see.

Had he stayed within the frame set by the teacher, the narrative would have been: BIG POWERFUL CONSERVATIVE GOVERNOR GETS TAUGHT LESSON BY TEACHER.

Predictably, liberal critics howled that his response had been "mean." That was all they could do, because Governor Christie had focused attention on a topic that the left did not want the public to think about. The new topic was, in essence, "Teachers know the pay scale when they agree to teach. If they want more money, they should go do something else." You know, personal responsibility and all that. The audience cheered in approval, and then Christie went on to focus on the extreme rhetoric of the union leadership. Game over.

The news media—other than Fox News—painted Christie's response in a negative light, but they were going to do that regardless of how he responded. But the viewers heard a perspective that they would not have heard if Christie had fallen into the traditional defensive trap.

If you were debating a liberal, which topic would you prefer to discuss, the one about poor, noble, underpaid teachers, or the one about personal responsibility and the tactics of liberal unions? Which topic do you think the liberal would want to talk about?

The first question you must always ask yourself when dealing with liberal accusations and demands is, "What is the topic the left wants to debate?" If the mainstream loses control of the topic, as we almost always do, the fight is over before it starts.

WHAT WE ASSUME

A second aspect of framing the narrative has to do with the assumptions that lie underneath the topic being debated. This aspect of the narrative is subtler, and because of its subtlety, mainstream Americans often fall into this trap without even noticing it.

For example, when a teachers' union takes the position that teachers are underpaid, there is an *unstated assumption* that others are responsible for any financial consequences of choosing to be a teacher. In essence, the union's unstated position is, "We'll decide what we want to do for a living, and then we'll decide what you should pay us to do it." If the union claims that a politician is hurting education because he wants to freeze teacher pay for a year or wants teachers to contribute to their benefits, the unstated assumption is that teacher pay and benefits determine the quality of our children's education.

By bringing those unstated assumptions to the surface, Governor Christie was able to challenge them openly.

Because the assumptions behind political positions are so often unstated, we tend to accept them as givens without even realizing it.

So you will find it tremendously helpful to consciously listen for those unstated assumptions and bring them to the surface.

Many of the unstated assumptions are embedded in the words we use. When we talk about raising taxes on "the rich" and raising taxes on "employers," we are usually talking about the same people. But depending on which term we use, we are working from subtly different assumptions about how they got their money and who suffers when the government takes more of it.

A common liberal claim about health care costs is that the government can, because of its size, buy medicine cheaper than private insurance or individuals. But note the unstated assumption that because the government *can* do something, it *should*. Government can also get volume discounts on cradles, food, housing, cars, guns, and grave plots. Does that mean that government should provide everything we need, from the cradle to the grave?

Exposing assumptions and bringing them to the surface is so critical to controlling the narrative that we will devote an entire section to these skills in a later chapter.

CONCLUSIONS AND IMPLICATIONS

The third aspect of framing the narrative has to do with the conclusions and implications that follow from the first two steps. For example, if Governor Christie had taken the bait, if he'd let the teachers' union define the topic and the assumptions for the discussion, he would have been forced into two damaging conclusions: (1) We'll have to figure out a way to pay teachers more (the union wins) or (2) Teachers will just have to remain underpaid (the mainstream looks cheap).

Thus, the political frame is determined by the topic that is the focus of discussion (and by the topics that are excluded), by the assumptions that are accepted as givens, and by the implications and conclusions.

FRAMING THE GM BAILOUT

Our example above was extended so that we could elaborate on several points, so let's do one more example that is shorter and more to the point. When General Motors was in trouble, the left had total control of the way the narrative was framed in the media and in the halls of Congress.

FOCUS OF ATTENTION

- Let's talk about the jobs that will be lost if we don't bail them out.
- Let's talk about the other industries that will be affected if GM fails.
- Let's *not* look at the reasons the company is in trouble, such as unsustainable commitments to the unions; just crop those out of the picture.
- Let's *not* look at the money trail from the unions back to the politicians who supported the bailout.
- Let's *not* talk about the fact that taxing well-run businesses to bail out poorly run businesses is unfair and hurts businesses that are better managed.
- Let's *not* look at the implicit message to large companies: "If you make good decisions, you reap the benefits. If you make bad decisions, you get to pass the consequences of your bad decisions on to the taxpayers."

UNSTATED ASSUMPTIONS

- It is the proper role of government to prop up businesses that make bad decisions.
- It is the proper role of government to decide which businesses succeed and which ones fail (because the government only bails out select businesses).
- The jobs will be lost forever (forget about the fact that better managed companies would buy those assets and put them to better use).

IMPLICATIONS AND CONCLUSIONS

- The government must do something and bail out GM.

The faster you can recognize the frame the left wants to use—the focus of attention, the unstated assumptions, and the implications—the better you will be able to take control of the narrative.

THE CORE TOOL: THE THREE Rs

In the heat of political exchanges, when the blood in our brains goes to the defensive centers, we often find that we don't think clearly. All the points that Limbaugh, Hannity, O'Reilly, or other conservative commentators have made about a particular issue will suddenly get lost in a fog of frustration. That compelling report you read from the Heritage Foundation will be a blank in your mind. In these moments, it helps to have a simple tool, one that you have practiced until you can use it easily, even in the heat of the political struggle. The tool is called the Three Rs:

- *Recognize the way the left wants to frame the narrative.*
- *Reframe the narrative to put the left on the defensive.*
- *Refocus the topic to drive the mainstream agenda.*

STEP 1: RECOGNIZE THE WAY THE LEFT WANTS TO FRAME THE NARRATIVE

The first step of the Three Rs is to *recognize* the box that the liberal wants to put you in.

We cannot overemphasize the importance of keeping your body in a relatively calm state during these encounters. Don't forget that breathing deeply and relaxing your muscles can calm the urge to react to accusations and absurdities coming from liberals. The calming effect of a deep breath combined with relaxing your muscles takes some of the visceral power out of the urge to defend and, more important, allows your mind to clear so that you can use the Three Rs. Even putting two or three seconds between the opening volley and your response can be enough time to break the defensive habit and take the liberal down a path that he does not want to go.

It is important to consciously label the frame that the left wants to use. Hear the words in your mind. Calling them out in your head can help you to see the trap the left is setting, and it also derails the impulse to respond to their narrative. Just ask yourself, "What is the debate the liberal wants to have?" and be aware of the answer.

- "She wants me to try to convince her that I'm not racist because I support secure borders."
- "He wants me to justify why I want to keep more of the money that I've worked for."
- "They want to rehash the one about rich people not paying their fair share of taxes."
- "She wants me to defend private health care."

When you clearly label the conversation that the liberals want you to have, it becomes obvious that no amount of evidence or reasoning will have any effect. The hardcore leftist's mind is already made up, and you will be defeated the moment you take the bait. To uninformed and misinformed voters who happen to be present, you will appear to be losing, because all the liberal has to do is to keep coming up with "Yes, but . . ." in response to any points that you make.

STEP 2: REFRAME THE NARRATIVE TO PUT THE LEFT ON THE DEFENSIVE

The second step is to reframe the issue or topic so that it puts the left in a negative light or on the defensive. So if they want you to try to prove to them that you think poor children should have access to health care, what do *you* want the topic to be? How about the impact of socialized medicine in other countries? Or, if the government can control health care, what other areas of our lives can the government take over? Liberals do not want to discuss those topics for obvious reasons.

This is where it helps to have a short list of popular liberal attacks and good reframes so that you can respond quickly and confidently. Fortunately, liberals are pretty predictable, so that isn't difficult.

The idea here is to offer a new premise that forces liberals to defend themselves and their positions. There are a number of ways to reframe the narrative, ranging from light reframes that are intended to mildly embarrass and discredit the liberal all the way to hard-hitting reframes that expose the hypocrisy and arrogance of the left for all to see.

The type of reframe that you use will depend on the circumstances, your goals, your opponent, and who else is listening.

As we cover these, just remember that the point of the reframe is the same in all cases: We want to divert the discussion from the path the liberal wants to take and put the liberal on the defensive. Let's start with lighter reframes and work our way up to the hard-hitting ones.

HUMOR AS A REFRAME

You might use the Humor Reframe when

- The setting is not appropriate for a serious discussion that could get heated and alienate uninformed and misinformed voters.
- You want to take a little wind out of the liberal's sails and make him look just a little silly, but without appearing hostile or mean.
- You have already used hard-hitting reframes and you need to keep the liberal on the rhetorical ropes without appearing to pummel him mercilessly.

The idea here is that a humorous response will often be the easiest and safest reframe. A funny retort turns the liberal's accusation or position into a joke at his expense.

Good-natured humor in response to liberal carping also makes you more credible and mature in the eyes of others. One of the classic political putdowns of all time was in the debate between Ronald Reagan and Jimmy Carter. When Carter kept repeating points that Reagan had already refuted, Reagan responded with a smiling, "There you go again!" Like a patient grown-up redirecting a petulant child, Reagan came across as the firm, mature, calm adult, while Carter came across as nettling. Carter could not have looked more at a loss in that moment if he had made an effort to do so. The debate was over and, with it, the election.

The best tone to use for a humorous reframe is one that is not hostile or belittling but still suggests that the liberal's claim is too silly to warrant a serious response.

- *"You guys really need to get some new material. Come on, let's talk about the real issue here."*
- *"Really? Solve the debt crisis by borrowing more money? I don't think so, and I'll bet you really don't either. Seriously, let's get back to some realistic solutions."*
- *"Well, you got me. If Obama were white, I wouldn't mind going on a waiting list to get an appendectomy or having to pull my own teeth like people do under socialized medicine."*

A playful grin at this point sends the message that you are not angry or hostile, that you know the left's position is more tactical than heartfelt, and that you assume anyone with good sense would know that as well. You have taken total control of both the spoken and unspoken discussions.

THE QUESTION REFRAME

Sometimes a leftist will hit you with a question that you know has an agenda behind it or will make a statement that seizes the high ground and dares all to come after them.

And sometimes your mind just goes blank. We run into this occasionally as guests on talk shows when a listener calls in with an out-of-left-field question. We talk politics for a living, and some leftists can still put our brains in vapor lock with their comments.

At such times, a subtle way to reframe the discussion is to ask a question. When you do so, you accomplish several things:

- You subtly break the underlying narrative that says the leftist will call the shots.
- If the question is a good one, you have set the stage to moving on to the topic that you want to discuss.
- You can find out more about the leftist's reasoning and assumptions.
- You buy yourself time to think.

LIBERAL: *"It's only fair that the rich should pay their fair share in taxes."*

It's tempting, when faced with such a statement, to try to point out tax rates, percentages of taxes paid by those at different income levels, and other facts that won't matter at all to a hardened leftist. But try something like this instead:

MAINSTREAMER: *"Well, let's take a husband and wife running a small business that employs ten people. Say they work about seventy hours each week, and their income is finally up to about $200,000. What do you think their fair share should be, and where do you think they will get the additional tax money?"*

The left cannot come up with a good answer for that one, because in their narrative "the rich" are cigar-smoking fat cats who never lift a finger and won't miss a few thousand here and there. The hardcore leftist will just accuse you of siding with "the rich," but the uninformed and misinformed who hear the discussion will get a more realistic picture of who the left is talking about and what happens to those employees when the government takes more money from their employer.

Try to use questions that expose underlying assumptions and basic principles.

Now consider a likely comment about the proper role of government in regulating greenhouse emissions:

LIBERAL: *"The government needs to take a larger role in reducing greenhouse emissions through regulation and taxing those who produce the most greenhouse gasses."*

Again, note that the leftist wants to lure you into a choice of "saving the planet" versus "refusing to give government the power it needs." Something like the following changes the whole direction of the discussion:

MAINSTREAMER: *"Our huge public school systems produce tons of greenhouse gasses as they bus students and as they heat and cool those thousands of buildings. And look at the greenhouse emissions from all the private vehicles that school employees use to get to and from work. Would you support a massive homeschooling initiative as a way to reduce greenhouse emissions?"*

No hardened leftist would favor homeschooling, regardless of any savings in greenhouse emissions, and so your question will have uncovered an inconvenient truth: The whole point of the climate change argument is to grow government. Greenhouse gasses are just the cover story. If they cannot think of a single way in which reducing government would reduce emissions, you have exposed the underlying assumption that government must grow at all costs. Either way, you will have seized control of the narrative.

THE ETIQUETTE LESSON REFRAME

You might use this one when

- You are outnumbered by liberals and the Humor Reframe might give them an excuse to turn violent.
- A liberal has started holding court in some setting where nobody really wants to discuss politics (e.g., Sunday school class or a dinner party).

Nothing galls the self-righteous like being lectured on righteousness. If you don't have good backup in the form of others who will join in some good-natured ribbing at the liberal's expense, you can fall back on the old "never discuss religion and politics."

MAINSTREAMER: *"This is a diverse group, and we have many points of view. I for one don't think it's appropriate to make comments that might be offensive to some."*

If you noticed that something along these lines is often used by liberals to shut up those they don't want to listen to, you are getting ahead of us. For now, the point here is that you have put the leftist in a bind: If she wants to maintain her veneer of respect for diversity, she has to get off her soapbox. If she keeps carping, just stay with the theme that "this isn't the place for that." (Caution: If you cannot keep a straight face, you cannot use the Etiquette Lesson Reframe.)

This one is a simple example of what we mean by taking back the culture. In our current culture, liberals feel free to hold court in a variety of situations in which their doing so makes others uncomfortable. They also feel free talking about the need to respect diverse points of view—when it is in their interest to do so. A response such as the one above, if repeated in thousands of encounters with liberals in thousands of situations, begins to set a new cultural norm: You do not have the right to force your leftist views on people any time you feel like it.

But there are times when a humorous response might seem flippant or might alienate the uninformed or misinformed voters that we want to win over. Or maybe the liberal missed the point of the humorous response—remember, hardcore leftist are a fairly humorless lot. Or maybe the liberals have been especially nasty and self-righteous in their attacks and a good verbal gut punch is called for.

THE DOUBLE BIND REFRAME

The Double Bind Reframe is a special case of putting liberals in a bind so that they lose no matter what they do. You might use this reframe when

- You know that the liberal you're dealing with is a true believer, one who subscribes to all of the liberal rhetoric and talking points.
- You want to hit fairly hard, but without appearing to do so.
- You need to stun the liberal long enough to collect your thoughts and refocus the discussion to suit your agenda.

A powerful technique is to answer one liberal position with another liberal position that contradicts it. This is the technique we used in our imaginary debate with a liberal environmentalist in Chapter 4

This technique works because leftist positions, statements, and accusations can so often be boiled down to "If I like it, it's good, and if I don't like it, it's bad." In the absence of any standard of reference other than their own likes and dislikes, leftists constantly take contradictory positions as they move from situation to situation and whim to whim. For examples, leftists use "appreciating diversity" to ensure that radical left-wing speakers are brought to college campuses, but then they switch to "stopping hate speech" as an excuse to ban any speakers they don't want to hear.

Once we realize that liberals use words arbitrarily as a means to get their way, we can use their own positions against them. In the process, we deny them their sense of superiority and highlight their hypocrisy for any uninformed or misinformed voters who might be present.

We call it a double bind because any direction the liberal takes will expose a contradiction in liberal positions. Most people expect to see some degree of consistency in a person's professed values and positions. When they see jarring contradictions, they smell hypocrisy.

The technique is simple. Just begin with a list of common liberal value statements, such as these:

- Diversity is good.
- Hate speech is bad.
- All morals are relative.
- It is wrong to impose your values on someone else.
- Artistic standards are a matter of personal preferences.
- Humans are products of blind evolution.
- We need strong women in society.

Then just pull one liberal value from the list and use it to challenge another liberal demand or position that contradicts it. It sounds complicated, but it's actually very easy.

Let's look at an example:

LIBERAL: *"It amazes me that anyone would think Michele Bachmann is qualified to be president."*

MAINSTREAMER: *"Well, a lot of people are threatened by strong women."*

When mainstreamers question the qualifications of liberal politicians who happen to be female—Hillary Clinton, for example—liberals avoid the question by saying that those people must be threatened by strong women. All we have done here is to use the liberal position against a liberal.

Now, liberals don't really believe that anyone challenging the qualifications of a woman is really threatened by strong women. They just use the claim as a stick to hit anyone who questions a *liberal* woman. They'd never dream that anyone would take their statement at face value and use it against them.

The key point with this technique is that you have taken the liberal from an offensive position to a defensive one, and that is the goal of any reframe.

Notice that it also works the other way around:

LIBERAL: *"I think some people just don't like Michele Obama because they are threatened by strong women."*

MAINSTREAMER: *"Yeah, just look at the way the news media treated Sarah Palin in the 2008 campaign or Michelle Bachmann in the 2010 campaign. The news media must really be threatened by those two."*

Once you practice this technique a few times, you will find that it tends to put leftists in a state of vapor lock for a few seconds, and that's all you need to take control of the topic being discussed.

A few more examples:

LIBERAL: *"I think talk radio is full of hateful speech that really should be regulated."*

MAINSTREAMER: *"In a diverse, multicultural society, we are all going to hear viewpoints that we don't like. We just all need to be more tolerant of those who are not like us."*

Let's try one more:

LIBERAL: *"It's time that we become a civilized society and outlaw all firearms."*

MAINSTREAMER: *"I respect your right to dislike firearms, but surely you would agree that you shouldn't impose your values on others."*

You wouldn't want to use this technique with the same liberal more than once per discussion. Watching a liberal scramble to make sense of contradictory liberal positions is like watching someone teasing a helpless kitten with the light from a laser pointer. At first the kitten's attempts to catch the light are funny, but eventually the person with the laser pointer starts to look a little cruel. So usually it is best to just expose one liberal contradiction at a time, reframe the narrative, and continue on to the next step, which is to change the topic to one that you want to discuss and the liberal doesn't.

There will be times, however, that you will need the verbal equivalent of a knockout punch, when you need to expose liberal hypocrisy and call it what it is.

THE INCONVENIENT TRUTH REFRAME

This reframe is most helpful when

- The left has been particularly vicious in their attacks, and anything less than a stunning response would look like a lack of conviction.
- Liberals have so overused a tactic, such as pulling the race card, that people are beginning to see through it.
- Liberals have been claiming the moral high ground even in the face of overwhelming evidence to the contrary and it is time to take the moral high ground back.

You can use this technique to deal with any number of leftist lies and distortions, so let's look at using it with some popular left-wing tactics.

SHREDDING THE RACE CARD

For decades, mainstream activists have dreaded the moment when the left pulls the race card. At first, the left used the race card as a diversion to keep opponents from criticizing a radical left-wing politician or race hustler who happened to be black. It worked so well, however, that they now use it to shut down all kinds of discussion of issues that have nothing to do with race, such as wanting to choose one's own doctor or controlling our borders.

The Inconvenient Truth Reframe differs from the previous ones in two ways:

- There is no subtle humor or irony here; you are directly calling out liberal hypocrisy and demanding an accounting for it.
- Because you want to confront liberal hypocrisy head-on, you need to personalize the issue wherever possible so that the liberal has to take a personal stand instead of spouting rhetoric.

The other reframes were one or two sentences, designed to take the liberal off her soapbox and give you control of the narrative. But because with this one you are calling liberal hypocrisy out in the open, and thus the liberal will be most threatened and angry, you will have to stand your ground so that there is no question in the mind of observers who is on the defensive. That may require several volleys with the liberal before you have the upper hand. Example:

LIBERAL: *"America is guilty of institutional racism."*

MAINSTREAMER: *"You are so right. Does anyone honestly believe that liberal politicians cannot see the damage their policies have done to black families?"*

LIBERAL: *"What? I was talking about the way white—"*

MAINSTREAMER: *"Sure, in the first part of the 1960s liberals could claim ignorance. I mean, the increase in illegitimacy rates had just started. But after decades, with an illegitimacy rate of over 70 percent, and with all the social problems that come with that, there is no excuse. If liberal politicians care so much about black people, why aren't they talking about that?*[59]*"*

LIBERAL: *"I must take exception to your use of the term 'illegitimacy.' That term implies that some family structures are inferior to others. Who are you to say—"*

MAINSTREAMER: *"Who benefits from the destruction of the black family? And who benefits from all the rhetoric that tells black Americans that they somehow don't belong? Black Americans are more churchgoing than any other group in America, but liberals would have us believe that black Americans celebrate a made-up holiday like Kwanzaa. Don't you think that black Christians should celebrate the same holidays as white Christians?"*

LIBERAL: *"I take personal offense at your hateful—"*

MAINSTREAMER: *"Well, let me just ask you this: Do you think black children are better off with a father who provides for them or without a father in the home?"*

LIBERAL: *"You cannot impose your definition of family—"*

MAINSTREAMER: *"I'm not talking about ivory tower theories here, I'm talking about real human beings who are being exploited by left-wing social policies. And you didn't answer my question: Do you think black children are better off with a father who provides for them or without one?"*

LIBERAL: *"I'm not going to impose my personal values—"*

MAINSTREAMER: *"The truth here is that the only people who benefit from liberal policies on race are the left-wing politicians who exploit black Americans, and the left has used the race card for years to keep that truth from getting out. The truth is tragic, but it is undeniable, and it is out now. We cannot turn back the clock to the days when we pretended not to notice what was going on."*

If you noticed the double-bind technique in the comment about "we cannot turn back the clock," you are well on your way to becoming a steely-eyed mainstream activist. For years, the left has accused conservatives of wanting to "turn back the clock," and now the liberal risks being accused of the same thing unless he agrees that it is time to move beyond the liberal policies that have caused so much damage.

Instead of running like frightened rabbits from the race card, mainstream politicians should be praying, "Lord, please let my opponent pull the race card today!"

Liberals cannot possibly defend the results of liberal social experimentation on black families. The issue of race rightfully belongs to the mainstream, the normal Americans who judge people by the content of their characters instead of the color of their skin. The only reason leftists get away with the race card is that mainstream Americans prefer to avoid unpleasantness. We treat politics like a polite civics class, and the left uses our decency to dominate us and to avoid taking responsibility for the damage that they do.

Enough is enough.

"LET'S PUT THE UNION FIRST"

Another inconvenient truth is that the left exploits, our children just as cruelly as they exploit issues of race. The teachers' unions raise money for left-wing politicians who return the favor by giving the unions more money and more power over our educational system. Of course, plenty of that money makes its way back to the liberal politicians in the form of contributions.

Just as liberals hide their self-serving policies behind noble-sounding racial rhetoric, they hide their agenda behind innocent children in schools.

Let's take a common example:

LIBERAL: *"Our teachers are underpaid and our children will suffer. We've got to have more money for education. That is, if we care about our children."*

MAINSTREAMER: *"Since when did the teachers' unions start accepting children as members?" [Knowing smile or chuckle here.]*

LIBERAL: *"What are you talking about? I'm talking about the desperate need—"*

MAINSTREAMER: *"We've got the most expensive school system on the planet and the results are dismal, and do you know why? Because the leadership of the teachers' unions only care about their own power, and they oppose anything that might actually raise educational standards."*

LIBERAL: *"I'm talking about making sure that our children—"*

MAINSTREAMER: *"Are you willing to fire incompetent teachers? Are you willing to allow vouchers so that parents can afford to get their children out of failing schools? Are you willing to get the political indoctrination out of our schools so that children can actually learn math and science?"*

LIBERAL: *"You don't understand. Some teachers have to bring their own pencils—"*

MAINSTREAMER: *"How do you justify spending billions on a political boondoggle like the Department of Education when we need more money for classroom teachers? And how much of that money makes its way back into the coffers of the left-wing politicians who are in the pocket of the teachers' union?"*

Again, there is nothing gentle or humorous here. The tone cannot and should not be mean or angry but should convey confidence and moral clarity. The idea is to shine the light of truth on left-wing hypocrisy *and* to put the leftist in question on the spot.

With these examples and with other issues, you will need to have your arguments in your mind and well rehearsed before you use this technique. Mainstream Americans, for the most part, do not like conflict, and when leftists get angry and your mouth gets dry and the blood in your brain goes to the limbic area, you will find it hard to remember your arguments. Research and rehearsal are the keys to continuing the volley.

And don't hesitate to interrupt, as we illustrated above. Just do so with passion and conviction. Interruption may be rude in civics class, but it works in politics. You don't want to appear rude to observers, though, so after the leftist has gotten angry, when the blood has gone to the defensive center of his brain, when you have hit him on several fronts, then be polite and let him have his say. He will hurt his own case far more than you ever could.

Always remember, the liberal's opening ploy is designed to take you into a narrative in which you are on the defensive. Watch for that ploy, recognize it, and then reframe the narrative to expose the left's hypocrisy.

Liberalism cannot stand the light of day, because every liberal position is ultimately about lording it over others.

STEP 3: REFOCUS THE TOPIC TO DRIVE
THE MAINSTREAM AGENDA

If you've used the first two steps in response to a liberal attack, you have successfully gained the upper hand and put the liberal on the defensive *on the issue that they raised.* That is, they attacked the mainstream as racist and you turned the tables to expose liberal hypocrisy on matters of race. But the topic is still race. Similarly, they demanded more money for "education" and you exposed their money-laundering scheme, but the topic is still funding for education.

That's fine if those are the topics that you as the mainstreamer want to pursue. But you now have the liberal off balance and disoriented, so it's a great time to advance your own agenda.

Reframing the issue puts liberals on the defensive on the topic that they have chosen. Refocusing the issue allows you to put the left on the defensive on topics of your choice. In practice, this step will often follow seamlessly after the second step.

Let's go back to the earlier example of Michele Bachmann's qualifications. The liberal was expecting you to defend her qualifications, and you reframed the topic to whether the liberal was threatened by Michele Bachmann. But what if you don't want to talk about Michele Bachmann? What if your real agenda is health care? It's simple. The liberal is off balance now, so just change the subject. So far, we have resisted the urge to defend Bachmann's qualifications and have reframed the issue to people being threatened by her:

LIBERAL: *"Do you really think Michele Bachmann is qualified to be president?"*

MAINSTREAMER: *"A lot of people are intimidated by strong women, so it makes sense that they would be threatened at the thought of her in the Oval Office."*

So now, while the liberal is still reeling, move on to health care:

MAINSTREAMER: *"But whether people are intimidated by her is not important to me. What's really important is that she will reverse the government's unconstitutional takeover of our health care system."*

The liberal now has several options, none of which are good. Continuing to question Bachmann's qualifications falls into the "threatened by strong women" trap. On the other hand, taking exception to the "threatened by strong women" idea violates liberal dogma. Or the liberal can defend the constitutionality of Obamacare.

Remember that the Recognize, Reframe, and Refocus model is a generic one. It can be applied to individual conversations, formal debates, and overall campaign strategies. Use your creativity and flexibly to handle your own struggles with the left. As long as you keep the liberal on the defensive, you are doing good work for your country.

FIRING FOR EFFECT: THE POWER OF THREES

But why stop at just one of your preferred topics? It's a good idea to have a short list of topics ready to launch. In pulling out your list, we recommend that you remember the power of threes. Lists packaged in threes seem to be especially memorable and powerful. Three points in a row seem to create a kind of rhythm that builds to a final point. Which of the following carries the most punch?

- *"This election is about jobs."*
- *"This election is about jobs and getting control of our borders."*
- *"This election is about jobs, getting control of our borders, and reining in our spending."*

You can almost hear the crowd's cheers after that last one. The first two statements are OK, but they don't build up to that big finish like the one packaged in threes.

Let's go back to the Michele Bachmann example. The mainstreamer scored by reframing the issue as "anyone who questions her qualifications must be intimidated by strong women," then seized the offensive by refocusing the issue onto the unconstitutional takeover of our health care system. So now imagine that the mainstreamer's response to the attack ended with three issues instead of just one:

> MAINSTREAMER: *"But whether people are intimidated by her is not important to me. What's really important is that she will reverse the government's unconstitutional takeover of our health care system, bring government spending under control, and restore some sanity to our immigration policy."*

Just a moment ago our liberal was trying to figure out how to respond to the point about being intimidated by strong women. Now he faces an attack on three fronts.

You could use these three issues (health care, spending, and immigration) as endings to any of the examples that we gave above. The mainstreamer's response in each case gains power from the rhythm of threes. Just to make the point, let's look at how to beef up the mainstreamer's response to the question of race:

> MAINSTREAMER: *"I think we do need to have a frank discussion about liberal exploitation of black people. Who has benefited from liberal policies that took the black out-of-wedlock birthrate from 6 percent to over 70 percent? Do liberals honestly believe that black children do not deserve to have fathers who provide for them?*
>
> *"But I also think we need to have frank discussions about other problems, such as the government's unconstitutional takeover of our health care system, the government's out of control spending, and the insanity of our border policy."*

You are now in full control of the narrative and the topic of discussion. And that's the whole point.

When refocusing the issue onto topics of your choice, choose topics that are especially relevant to any uninformed or misinformed voters who might be present. The idea is to pick topics that emphasize the distance between the positions of the radical left and those of the audience. For example, where unemployment is high, be sure to point out how liberal policies have wrecked the ability of businesses to hire. If there has been some kind of scandal involving a local school, be sure that something like "cleaning up the mess in our educational system" is one of your points.

If you are a candidate or an activist and you are interviewed on television, refocus any hostile question from a reporter onto three topics that will most highlight the difference between most viewers and the liberals.

REPORTER: *"There have been numerous charges that the Tea Party movement is extremist. How do you respond?"*

MAINSTREAM ACTIVIST *[chuckling]: "Oh, the radical left screams 'extremism' whenever they don't want to talk about the issues that are important to the taxpayers, and mainstream Americans aren't falling for that. But seriously, we have to get control of our insane spending, we have to reduce the tax barriers to job creation, and we want to see some sanity in our homeland security policies. The Tea Party has finally given the people who pay for our government a chance to have a voice in that government."*

Awareness of your intended audience is essential if you are to help inform and convert the uninformed and misinformed who are open to reason and evidence. And as long as liberals are on the defensive and not firing at the mainstream from some phony moral high ground, your reason and evidence will be more appealing to those swing voters. You will come across as confident and the left will come across as defensive and trying to pull a fast one.

HARNESSING THE POWER OF ANGER

Though the "news" media tell stories about angry Tea Partiers, the reality is that anger is the signature liberal emotion. The vapors of anger waft from the liberal institutions like the odor of cheap booze from a flophouse.

Liberals are almost always angry about something, and they are experts at getting their followers riled up, especially before an election. Angry people vote, and liberals know that. And mainstream Americans tend to try to placate angry liberals. That has been the pattern of the Appeasement Cycle.

Anger is a complex emotion. If we don't have some of it, we seem to lack normal human passion, especially about things that are unjust or unfair. On the other hand, if we have too much of it, we can appear out of control and immature.

For political purposes, there are three key points for the mainstream to understand when harnessing the power of anger.

1. *You want to present yourself as cool-headed, rational, mature, and caring.*

Mainstream voters will not respect someone who comes across as angry and bitter. That is why we usually suggest a good-natured, humorous response to liberal attacks as a first choice, as if the attack just really cannot be taken too seriously. That leaves the liberal looking like he is not in control of his emotions, and that hurts his credibility. Remember Howard Dean's infamous "I Have a Scream" speech? He went from left-wing idol to left-wing flake in one outburst. So, with one exception, leave the anger to the liberals.

The one exception, the one situation in which people *want* to see someone in a position of influence respond with passion that borders on anger is when that person is speaking on behalf of their group in a situation in which their group has been wronged. Remember George W. Bush standing in the rubble of the World Trade Center with the workers chanting "USA, USA, USA"? Bush responded, "I hear you." Then came the statement that struck just the right tone for the situation: "And the people who brought down these buildings are going to hear from all of us soon!" His tone conveyed righteous anger in the form of resolve and conviction, but he did not for even a moment appear to be at the mercy of his emotions. It was just what the physically and emotionally drained workers needed to hear from the president of a country under attack.

Contrast the tone of that moment with the tone of the John McCain campaign in 2008. McCain came across more like an applicant for an accounting job than a passionate defender of a country under attack by sixties radicals and their philosophical descendants. The only question leading up to the vote was whether McCain could demoralize the Republican base faster than Obama could mobilize them.

He did.

So when you're speaking on behalf of the mainstream about wrongs done by the radical left, it is fine to show passionate intensity appropriate to the situation. Show indignation at the injustice done to the taxpayers of the country. People need to know that you are one of them, that you are on their side, and that you share their frustrations. Think in terms of conviction, moral clarity, resolve, and a firm commitment to speaking the truth. But you never, ever want to appear angry or to be ruled by your emotions. Leave that to the liberals. Balance is the key.

2. *You want to trigger the indignation of the voters and channel it toward defeating liberals.*

The gradual liberal undermining of our nation became a frontal assault in 2008, and the mainstream giant was awakening and "filled with a terrible resolve." That is, the normal, righteous, totally appropriate anger of the mainstream was kindled.

When laws are made that do not reflect the values of the culture, those laws are by definition tyrannical. If anyone has a right to feel indignation and resentment, it is mainstream Americans, whose values and wishes have been consistently ignored and insulted by an increasingly arrogant and unrepresentative government. If anyone has a right to feel resentment, it is the American people who heard Barack Obama's disdain for them as "clinging to their guns and religion" while bowing before foreign leaders. If anyone has a right to be resentful, it is the taxpayers whose money pays liberal politicians to insult us.

There are three especially powerful triggers of resentment, and you should make full use of them as you practice the Three Rs technique:

- *Threats to resources:* Emphasize the left's constant attempts to take more of our earnings.
- *Threats to autonomy:* Draw attention to the ways in which liberal policies deny citizens the ability to make choices for themselves.
- *Perception of unfairness:* Hypocrisy reeks of unfairness. The more you expose leftist hypocrisy, the less credibility the left will have.

3. *If the left gets angry, let them.*

We have discussed limbic surges, those moments when the brain's emotional areas are triggered and the capacity for clear thinking is diminished. This is the principle behind the classic movie courtroom scene when incessant pressure from the defense attorney results in an emotional confession from the *real* killer: "Yes, yes, yes, I did it. I killed him. Me. I killed him. And I'm glad. Glad, you hear me? Ha ha ha ha ha ha!"

A bit dramatic, maybe, but it makes the point that under emotional pressure, people say and do things that work against them. No matter how skilled you become at our techniques, you'll never get a leftist to break down on camera and blurt out, "Yes, yes, yes, I hate America and I hate your stupid Constitution!" But you can do the next best thing. When the scenarios don't play out the way they expect, when the mainstream refuses to debate on the left's terms, liberals are going to be in new territory. When they are on the defensive, their anger is more likely to come out, along with heaven knows what else! And their credibility will suffer accordingly. Your job is to put them on the defensive and keep them there. But always be careful. If liberal anger and resentment exposes their real agenda, that's good. But you don't want to give them an excuse to get violent.

LEFTIST ANGER VERSUS RIGHTEOUS INDIGNATION

There is a difference between righteous indignation and anger as a *manipulative tool*. When taxpayers are trying to address a $15 trillion debt and they hear liberals referring to the Tea Party as "terrorists," those taxpayers feel righteous indignation. Leftists, on the other hand, use anger to manipulate their followers for the purpose of giving liberals the power that they so desperately crave.

Angry voters go to the polls regardless of the weather, regardless of the length of the lines, and regardless of what is on television. Angry voters vote with a purpose. The people in America who have a right to be indignant are the disenfranchised mainstream taxpayers and the victims of liberal exploitation. Mainstream candidates and activists need to trigger that indignation and channel it into productive political action.

That is where the three common anger triggers come into play. When it's pointed out to people that their resources are being taken and wasted or even used against their best interests, those people will be motivated to take appropriate political action. When it is pointed out to people that their freedom of choice, their options in education, health care, and other areas of life are increasingly restricted, their righteous anger will be kindled. And when the gross unfairness of liberal policies is made evident to people, they will not just vote, they will be motivated voters who would not sit out the election for any reason.

The Reframe and Refocus steps in our Three Rs tool are logical places to use the three anger triggers. In so doing, you will not only accomplish the purpose of the Three Rs—to deflect the liberal attack and put the liberal on the defensive—you will also help to educate any neutral observers about what's going on in our political world. Consider the following from a hypothetical campaign debate:

> LIBERAL: *"My opponent has refused to support badly needed funding for our underpaid teachers. Will you commit in front of these people to change your position?"*

> MAINSTREAMER *[chuckling]*: *"I will commit to putting the taxpayers' money where it belongs: in the classroom instead of in the pockets of overpaid bureaucrats. I would like my opponent to tell these taxpayers just what a diversity coordinator does to earn a six-figure salary!"*

Note the triggers that the mainstream candidate used. "Wasted tax money" seems unfair to begin with, and it also drains resources from taxpayers. The liberal has been put on the defensive, which was an important goal in itself. But neutral voters in the audience would also have a question planted in their minds about the fairness of having their tax money go to pay a diversity coordinator, especially while claiming that teachers are underpaid. If the mainstream politician in this example wanted to play for keeps, the next step would be to refocus the issue with something like the following:

> MAINSTREAMER: *"But the biggest problems facing us now are left-wing policies that have driven employers from our area, raised the taxes on working families, and added layers of bureaucracy to an already bloated government."*

Note the anger triggers in the Refocus step above. "Driving employers away" limits employment options and threatens resources. "Raising taxes on working families" is a clear threat to resources. And "adding bureaucracy" when employers are leaving town and taking jobs with them just seems downright unfair. In this case, the audience should see clearly that they have been victimized by liberal policies, and they should be able to make up their mind which candidate has their best interests at heart.

BALANCING NEGATIVES AND POSITIVES

In using the Three Rs technique, as you expose liberal hypocrisy and focus the righteous resentment of voters on the damage done by the left, you run the risk of coming across as "negative," even if you show appropriate passion and do not appear angry or out of control.

A good principle to keep in mind is that people seem to weigh negative comments more heavily than positive ones. If you balance one "attacking" comment with one "solution," you are likely to be seen as engaged in "negative campaigning." A good rule of thumb is that for each hard-hitting comment, you need to make several others—maybe three to five—that would be seen as positive. These could be proposed solutions for problems, recognition of the efforts of others, and so on.

Liberals don't balance negative and positive comments, because they don't have to. Liberals start negative and stay negative, and the response of the news media is to ask mainstream politicians how they plead to the charges. But when mainstreamers point out facts that liberals want to keep quiet, leftist politicians and their media echo chambers whine about "negative campaigning," and many uninformed and misinformed voters unthinkingly look for any signs of "negativity" from the mainstream. So be very deliberate in balancing hard-hitting comments with caring language and positive solutions.

That is the point of our fifth principle.

PRINCIPLE 5: HIT HARD AND SUE FOR PEACE.

A good technique is to hit hard at a point of liberal hypocrisy and then immediately move the conversation toward positive solutions. Hit hard, then seize that moment of confusion on the left's part to take the high road and call for an end to all the negativity and demand positive solutions instead. It goes like this:

MAINSTREAMER: *"It's nothing short of rank hypocrisy that liberal politicians would force the failed socialist health care system on mainstream*

Americans while exempting themselves, their own families, and their cro-
nies. If it's good enough for the taxpayers who have to foot the bill, why
isn't it good enough for the liberals who wanted socialized medicine in
the first place?

"But liberal hypocrisy is old news and I don't want to dwell on it. The
people of this country live every day with the problems caused by the left's
failed policies, and they want to hear positive solutions. I want to focus
our efforts on restoring the right of free Americans to choose their own
health care, on using market solutions to make the best health care in
the world even better, and on making sure that future generations enjoy
health care free of government bureaucracy.

"And I challenge my opponent to leave off the name-calling and talk
about these positive solutions. To do otherwise insults the intelligence of
the people."

Notice the one-two-three rhythm at the end and how the momentum of the positive comments seems to build. Also notice the advantage of hitting hard and then calling for an end to all the negativity.
We have just pointed out liberal hypocrisy, which people have a need
to know about, and we have also positioned our statement as "above
the fray" of negative campaigning. A liberal candidate who counter-
attacks after the above statement would be begging for a scolding
about "negative campaigning" that "insults the intelligence" of people
who are ready for "positive solutions."

If this technique sounds like hitting below the belt, always remember: This is what happens in the political ring.

The only referee is the voter.

9

FILLED WITH A TERRIBLE RESOLVE

The birth and rapid growth of the Tea Party movement tells us that the mainstream giant has been awakened by the left's arrogance and corruption. The only question is whether that giant has been filled with sufficient resolve to do what must be done. We know now that we can no longer win elections and then go home. We have to take our country back from the culture up. We have to restore the character that once made us great. There is no longer any such thing as "between elections."

If the mainstream giant has indeed been "filled with a terrible resolve," we will have a long struggle on our hands. But in the end, the liberal minority cannot prevail against our numbers.

PRINCIPLE 6: DRIVE THE MAINSTREAM AGENDA THROUGH THE CULTURE AND THE GOVERNMENT.

We have argued that political power is like an iceberg, with the formal institutions of government represented by the visible tip and the cultural institutions represented by the larger portion beneath the surface. The left's strategy has been to dominate the government by dominating the culture, and it is clear that no electoral victory will matter until mainstream America once again dominates the culture on which government rests.

In addition to common targets such as taxes and governmental spending, then, grassroots groups should target the educational system, news and information, and other cultural institutions in their local communities. We will give an extended example in this chapter of methods for addressing liberal bias in a local school. These methods can also be used for targeting other liberal strongholds, ranging from a biased newspaper to liberal dogma in a local museum display.

You can adapt the methods to any number of political efforts. But you will have little success on your own. Though mainstream Americans are not political joiners by nature, we will only exercise power if we leverage our tremendous numerical advantage over the far left.

The enemy who occupies our institutions will not fear you alone. But that enemy will fear you and a few million of your closest friends.

MANAGING THE MOVEMENT

There are two essential tasks in building a political movement. One is getting mainstreamers to join together in groups such as the Tea Party movement or other grassroots groups working to return the nation to constitutional government. These groups tend to be loosely organized and totally dependent on the energy and commitment of volunteers. Activists in these groups will play a major role in taking control of the narrative in the culture at large.

The other task is to get mainstreamers into positions of power within the established institutions. That means getting mainstream candidates elected to school boards, appointed to local and state commissions and task forces, on library and museum boards, and into elected offices at every level. If it's public, it's political. And if it's private, it's political too.

No Enemies on the Right

A motto of the left's Long March has been "There are no enemies on the left." This simple dictum has been tremendously helpful for the liberal minority. They rarely turn on one of their own, no matter what crimes or corruption may be uncovered.

Mainstreamers, however, will splinter over principles at a moment's notice. It is harder to hold our movement together because of the tendency to break into smaller and smaller groups over some real or imagined difference. We have to decide now: Who is a greater threat to our liberty and to that of our children, someone who opposes the left but has an occasional idea that we do not like, or the leftists who would spend us into economic oblivion?

We suggest that you have no real enemies on the right. Let's break the liberals' Long March first, and then we can squabble at our leisure about libertarian versus traditional views, free trade versus economic nationalism, interventionist versus noninterventionist foreign policies, and so on.

Organizing Essentials

It is beyond our purpose here to go into depth about how to develop and manage a movement with a large number of people. If you are new to political activism, however, a few basic points about group dynamics can help you to make sense of some of the things you will see. These pointers would apply when working with any grassroots organization that relies on volunteer efforts.

SIMPLE THEME

You will need a rallying theme that is clear, simple, and memorable. The Tea Party movement attracts people who are concerned about excessive spending and excessive government. But there are many other grassroots groups and established organizations working on a variety of mainstream concerns. If your passion is to correct the left-wing bias in textbooks, for example, you will be able to find other parents and taxpayers who are concerned about that issue. And you don't have to start from scratch. Somebody out there already knows quite a bit about your particular area of concern. A little research and networking can bring you together with those people who have the skills and resources you need to be effective.

SIMPLE LEADERSHIP STRUCTURE

"Leaderless groups" are a myth. Regardless of the size of the group, there will have to be a small number of people guiding it and, frankly, doing much of the actual work. It is a rare group that spreads the work equally, so don't get too distracted by concerns about who is pulling the wagon and who isn't. It's the national wagon we need to worry about, and right now close to half of all voters don't pay any federal income taxes at all. Keep a consistent focus on threats to resources, freedom of movement, and the unfairness of liberal policies to keep your group energized.

LEVERAGE TECHNOLOGY

Use digital resources such as Facebook, Twitter, and other social networking tools to rapidly expand your membership and communicate about important events. It is notoriously difficult to get mainstreamers to volunteer for any political activity—unlike the left's union demonstrators, we're not getting paid to be there—so you have to do everything possible to make it easy for people to join the cause.

CREATE THE IMPRESSION OF A FLURRY OF ACTIVITY

One of our political mentors used to point out to his protégés that the impression of a flurry of activity creates a sense of inevitability, and that saps opponents' morale. Frequent letters to the editor, mentions in the news media, flooding the talk shows, and high-profile activities create the impression of viability and momentum.

Remember, the news media will film ten liberal activists from camera angles that exaggerate their numbers and play up their passion. On the other hand, the liberal media will attempt to ignore or downplay the size of any mainstream movement, so our numbers have to be so stunning, so overwhelming, that we cannot be ignored.

MULTIPLY THE BENEFITS OF INVOLVEMENT

Find ways to make working with your group not only politically gratifying but also beneficial for social and business interests. One of the best rewards for involvement in mainstream grassroots movements is meeting others who share your concerns. Mainstream activists are the backbone of the country; these are people you would want to know even if you weren't trying to save the country.

It should go without saying that mainstreamers should direct our business to other mainstreamers whenever possible, and that we should use our network to refer business to other mainstreamers in the movement. Real estate, dry cleaning, printing, car repair, accounting—whenever you can, take your business to those who are working for your freedom. This is especially important when we stop to think that the careers or businesses of mainstream activists might suffer as liberals retaliate.

Young people involved in mainstream grassroots work are especially vulnerable to the influence of peers who have soaked up liberal dogma in school. Make sure young activists meet peers who are in the mainstream. In the next chapter we will offer educational strategies to keep young people in the mainstream even as they are immersed in liberal institutions.

STAY INFORMED, BUT DON'T REINVENT THE WHEEL

The Internet and social media have given us a tremendous ability to share information and best practices in a short period of time. There are excellent online resources for those who want to get involved politically.

Here is a short list of some we have found tremendously helpful. Using only these resources, new activists can go from concerned to equipped in a very short time. Seasoned activists will deepen their knowledge and broaden their toolkit.

Build your own list and share it with your grassroots group. Always include information about our founding principles and our founding documents:

- Founders' Truth: At *founderstruth.org*, you will find an excellent resource with a specific focus on the Judeo-Christian foundations of our republic. These foundations have been deliberately targeted by the left, and we cannot defend them if we do not know the truth.

- The Frederick Douglass Foundation: The old civil rights movement has become a wholly owned subsidiary of liberal Big Government. The Frederick Douglass Foundation (*frederick douglassfoundation.com*) provides a mainstream alternative to civil rights, not only from a racial perspective, but in a way that applies to all Americans concerned about liberty. The approach is specifically and unapologetically Christian.

You will also need information resources about pending legislation and policy issues:

- Heritage Foundation: We check *heritage.org* on a daily basis and get daily e-mail updates as well. You'll find everything from in-depth policy analysis and recommendations to up-to-the-minute assessments of pending legislation.

- Intellectual Takeout: Though it will be especially useful for students immersed in liberal propaganda, *intellectualtakeout.org* is an excellent resource for anyone who wants to understand a wide range of political and economic issues from a perspective that values individual liberty.

Because the left owns the news media for the most part, you will need resources to combat bias and omissions:

- Accuracy in Media: Mainstream activists need to be aware of the manner in which the left-wing media spins the national narrative. Accuracy in Media (*aim.org*) works tirelessly to expose distorted and inaccurate coverage and strives for fair and objective coverage.
- Media Research Center: The MRC offers in-depth analysis of liberal bias in the media. We also find Cybercast News Service (*cnsnews.com*) to be an excellent resource for unbiased and unfiltered news reporting.
- Newsbusters: *Newsbusters.org* provides up-to-the-minute exposure of liberal bias in news coverage.

Finally, you will need resources for managing the practical details of organizing and managing a political movement:

- AnyStreet: An excellent resource for conservative community organizing, *anystreet.org* provides practical tools to support mainstream activists from first gear to high gear. Those new to political activism will find this an especially helpful resource. As it says on their website, "The president of *Modern Conservative* jokingly calls AnyStreet '*ACORN, without the evil.*'"

Please note that these are just a few of hundreds of outstanding resources to help you stay informed. Our intention is to give you a starter kit, and to emphasize the need to have resources in several different areas. As you find other resources for mainstream activists, be sure to share them with your group.

STAGES OF GROUP FORMATION

Any group that you join or organize will likely go through some predictable stages. Your awareness of these stages and the challenges you are likely to face in each can help you avoid common problems. Though there are formal models of group or team formation, we find the following conceptualization simple and useful.

One word of warning: groups do not go through these stages in smooth steps, and changes in membership can raise questions that had already been resolved. Even so, it can help grassroots activists to understand basic points of group formation so that we don't fall apart when we hit predictable bumps.

THE "WHAT" STAGE

To understand the behavior of a group in the early stages of formation, think about a first date. Behavior early on is superficial and nice, and the natural tendency is to avoid topics or issues that could cause unpleasantness. When first attending a group, people want to know the answer to several basic questions:

1. What is the purpose of the group? What are its goals?
2. What does this group do? Do I want to participate in that?
3. What's in it for me? What benefits could I experience if I join in?
4. What will be expected of me as a member?

Good leaders of grassroots efforts in this stage provide a compelling message about the purpose of and need for the group. They are skilled at welcoming people and ensuring that people have a chance to meet and interact, to build the social bonds that will help the group in the next stage.

Skilled leaders will pay particular attention to the question of how new participants can benefit by involvement. The desire to do something about the corruption and abuse of power in Washington will get people to their first meeting, but progress on those goals will take time and will be piecemeal. Enjoyable social and business connections are common motivators that keep mainstreamers involved even when the goal is huge and progress is slow.

Because of left-wing dominance in cultural institutions, our experience is that most mainstreamers are relieved to find out that they are not the only ones who think liberalism is dangerous. We have even had mainstreamers tell us that they wondered if they were crazy for thinking that liberal policies seemed racist, that bailouts for the ostensible purpose of "saving jobs" were actually political payoffs, and that the easy promises of socialism were false promises. It tells us quite a bit about the power of our cultural institutions that 20 percent of the population can make the other 80 percent feel alone and isolated. The message that "you are not alone" is a powerful one for people who are first testing the waters of political involvement.

THE "HOW" STAGE

Because grassroots groups are volunteer in nature, the power structure is far subtler than that in organizations of paid workers. Early on, the organizers and early joiners are likely to be people who are energetic, active, and vocal. Once individuals make the personal decision that they want to belong to and participate in a group, then, in order to function effectively and efficiently, questions of how the group will meet its goals become paramount:

1. How will we make decisions?
2. How will we divide the work?
3. How will we handle disagreements?
4. How will we handle problems?

This stage of development can feel like the group has hit a speed bump. Just remember, this is perfectly normal and there are ways to get past any issues that arise.

The most common problems we see with mainstream grassroots organizations are differences of opinion regarding decision-making and frustration with the unequal distribution of work. As we said earlier, it is not our purpose here to offer detailed instructions on managing grassroots organizations, but we can offer an observation: These two issues are almost inevitable. Somebody will say, "Who decided we would issue this press release?" and somebody else will say, "Why can't we get people to pitch in with this?" It is these two issues that often cause people to get discouraged and leave the group. There are no easy or quick answers for handling these issues, other than to realize that they are normal challenges of group work.

The leader's goal is to use these issues when they arise to clarify the group's norms about handling those issues. Different groups will reach different norms about decision-making processes and how to handle the inevitable disparity in work among members. As long as the group can agree on those norms, that will help keep the group refocused on its real mission. After the first speed bumps about decision-making, for example, you might agree on a procedure for issuing press releases. The point is not to turn the group into a bureaucracy, but simply to have some basic agreements that minimize internal conflict and focus the group on the real enemy.

You will not be able to make everyone happy, so accept that. A few people may drop out over various issues, and that's normal. Such exits do not have to be bitter or leave hard feelings. We do not need any animosity or factions among those working to restore America. The goal is for people who want to get involved to find their place in the movement.

As long as your group develops working norms that allow you to stay focused on your mission and not on internal conflicts, you will minimize drop-outs. If you fail to reach working norms, however, you will be distracted by constant internal conflicts.

Just put the real issues on the table when you see these problems, remind the group that they are normal issues, restate your larger mission, and then ask the group to reach some basic agreements so that you can move on.

THE "WOW" STAGE

Your group will have to have satisfactorily weathered the first two stages to have a reasonable chance at the third. In this stage of group formation, the group is clear on its purpose and has evolved ways of doing the work that work for everyone. Those whose needs and preferences were not met by your group will have gone somewhere else, and that is as it should be in a grassroots effort.

It is in this stage that the group can identify and communicate about issues that are central to your mission, such as adoption by a local school of a notoriously biased history text. Now that everyone knows who is on point for what actions, the group has the potential to start acting like a political giant.

THE CAMEL'S NOSE STRATEGY

The idea here is that the camel gets just its nose under the tent. There is protest from those inside the tent at first, but they get used to it. Then the camel moves in a little more. Again there is protest, and again those in the tent get used to having more of the camel inside their tent. Eventually, the camel is sitting inside the tent.

If this sounds like the strategy that the left used to get inside the tent of our institutions, you are right. The difference is that we have a much larger camel.

Let's take a simple example to illustrate the method, one that you can adapt to suit your goals. Suppose you and a group of concerned mainstream parents want to address a particularly egregious example of liberal bias in a textbook. The idea is to exact *some* concession from the liberals without making any concession yourself. It doesn't matter how small the concession, as long as the left loses ground.

When you have exacted some small concession, such as getting the school to accept supplementary materials with a more mainstream perspective, let the left feel that they have won. Let them celebrate.

They have so much power now that a small concession should not feel like much to them. The longer they go without realizing that their power is eroding, the better. No concession is too small, as long as they lose ground and we don't.

The principles below will apply regardless of the venue. Your group might be contesting bias in a text used by a local school, opposing a tax increase proposed by your local government, protesting biased coverage by a local paper or news show, demanding more balanced presentations in a local museum, or pushing a long-term legislative strategy. The techniques will be the same.

HAVE A DEMAND GOAL AND A COMPROMISE GOAL

In the case of a biased textbook, you are fighting an entrenched liberal enemy, so be aware that you will not get what you want. Go ahead and be bold in your original demand. For example, your group can demand that the school drop the biased textbook and buy no more textbooks from that publisher. You will not win that one. So be prepared to "compromise" as a sign of your good intentions and open-mindedness. The compromise is your real goal.

In any public statements, emphasize your willingness to reach a compromise that would be "fair to all concerned." Seize the moral high ground. Without saying so directly, create the impression that refusal to compromise is stubborn and grossly unfair.

Make sure that liberals lose ground in the compromise and that the mainstream loses nothing, not an inch. For example, the compromise could be that, say, all history courses will offer *The Politically Incorrect Guide to American History*[60] as supplemental reading, and that a Fairness and Accuracy Committee of parents will be established to review textbooks and make nonbinding recommendations. That would, of course, have been the real goal all along, the camel's nose under the tent. You may have to scale back on your compromise goal, and that's fine—as long as the left loses ground and you gain ground.

Then, once they've accepted that, start work on your next demand.

Maybe the supplemental reading could later become required reading under the rubric of "critical thinking." Maybe the nonbinding recommendations from the parents' committee would eventually require a publicly recorded vote by school board members.

Or maybe your group could suggest that the school board invite Dr. Thomas Sowell or Dr. Walter Williams as guest speakers during Black History Month. When it turns out that their fees are too high (that will be one of the left's excuses), you can settle for having the school buy their books in bulk and make them available to students—available this year, but eventually required. When liberals on the school board object that the books cost too much, get local businesses to provide the books to the school for free as a way of "giving back to the community." If liberals complain about the mainstream nature of the books, reframe that as ingratitude about local businesses trying to help local schools.

And pray that some leftist on the school board objects to Sowell or Williams on political grounds. For liberals to admit that the criterion for inclusion in Black History Month is political rather than racial would be a slow pitch right over the plate. Heaven help us if we can't knock the cover off that one.

Frame the Debate in Your Favor

Remember that you want to seize the offensive and put the liberals on the defensive. Be very clear how you are going to frame the issue before you make your first public comment. The left will try to frame any discussion of textbooks this way: "Who should control the content of textbooks—subject matter experts or right-wing extremists with a political agenda?"

So deny them that debate. What is the debate *you* want to have? In this case, "Should textbooks reflect the values of mainstream Americans who pay for the textbooks or those of ivory-tower academics?" The particular issue will determine the frame that you use, but the underlying rule is to frame the issue as "mainstream citizens versus liberals." There are more of us than there are of them.

CONTROL THE UNSTATED ASSUMPTIONS

In framing any debate or conflict with liberals, be careful how you frame those things that are to be debated versus those things that are assumed. This distinction is subtle, and therein lies the power. For example, if you say, "This presentation of American history strikes me as *radical*," the issue to be debated is whether the presentation is, in fact, radical. That isn't so bad, in that the liberals would at least be defending their own ground. But there is some burden of proof on you to defend your claim.

On the other hand, if you framed the issue as, "Using a textbook to push a radical position just doesn't seem fair to the taxpayers," then you have treated it as *assumed* that the contents are radical; the radical nature of the content is a *given*. Now the only issue to be debated is whether having such radical content is *fair*. Anyone other than a liberal who hears the comment will likely be predisposed to question the fairness of pushing a radical viewpoint in a textbook. Liberals would now have two unpleasant, defensive options: They can argue that the content isn't radical—in which case you win by drawing public attention to the questionable content—or they can attempt to take the position that it is fair to use taxpayers' funds to push a political agenda that most taxpayers wouldn't like.

As long as you control the frame for the issue, you should be magnanimous. Remember to hit hard wherever possible without appearing to do so: "I'm sure that our own local school board would not approve of the radical spin in the examples we've cited. They're very busy, but I'm sure they will appreciate being made aware of this problem."

CONTROL THE LANGUAGE TO CONTROL THE NARRATIVE

Because liberals use words for their impact rather than to communicate ideas, they have developed an arsenal of very powerful words. Now it's up to you to use those words against them. The issue in textbooks is one of *fairness*. The issue of charter schools and vouchers is one of *choice*. Parents redressing their grievances with the local educational authorities are *speaking truth to power*. Homeschooling helps to meet *diverse student needs*.

Using their own language against liberals is important for two reasons. One is that, when the mainstream uses those words, the words will actually correspond to reality, so your comments will sound sensible to others in the mainstream, and especially to uninformed and misinformed voters. The second is that it's fun to watch the veins pop out in the liberals' heads when confronted with their own hypocrisy. They will not be at their best when the blood flows to their limbic system, and you can use that to your advantage.

Some examples of deliberate use of language:

1. Any and all tax cuts should be described as "benefiting working families."
2. Any and all tax increases should be described as "sapping the hard-earned resources of working families" and cramping "job creation."
3. Never refer to "redistribution of wealth." Some of the uninformed may harbor jealousy toward the "wealthy." Any redistribution scheme should be described as a "redistribution of *earnings*." Few people, even the uninformed, support having their earnings taken from them.
4. If liberals propose reform, they are up to something. Don't fall into the trap of opposing reform. You are not opposed to health care reform; you are opposed to the takeover of our health care system by left-wing bureaucrats.
5. Avoid criticizing unions. Position your statements as concerned about "corruption of union bosses" and how that corruption is unfair to hardworking rank-and-file union members.
6. Never criticize teachers. In your statements, make a clear distinction between "hardworking teachers" and "the radical teachers' unions" or "the federal bureaucrats who make it so hard for good teachers to do their jobs." If we can get the federal

government's nose out of our schools, our teachers can get back to teaching.

7. Corporations or companies or businesses are all "employers."

8. The relationship between black Americans and liberal political groups should be consistently described as "exploitation." The race card will be played in every election, so why not be the one to play it? Bemoan the sad fact that "white liberals exploit black Americans to build their own power base." Another good one: "It would be tragic for white liberals to do to Hispanic families what they have done to black families." The difference between mainstreamers playing the race card and liberals playing the race card is that mainstreamers will be telling the truth and exposing an evil by doing so.

9. Frame any issue as pitting liberals against mainstream Americans. Synonyms for "liberal" are "the left wing," "radicals," "hardliners," "leftists," "rich liberals," "limousine liberals," "the far left," "left-wing extremists," "big government," and so on. Synonyms for "mainstream" are "taxpayers," "citizens," "working Americans," "normal Americans," "the voters," "the American people," and so on.

FIND THREE RALLYING THEMES FOR YOUR CAUSE

Remember the power of threes. Find three particularly egregious examples of bias and hammer those home in every encounter with the left and in every communication. Make those three examples the talk of your town. Whenever there's an opening for discussion of local news or even gossip, you can insert, "Have you heard about the textbook scandal? It's unbelievable some of the stuff they're putting in kids' heads." Remember, "unfairness" is a major anger trigger, and abusing one's professional standing to indoctrinate children is the height of unfairness.

If the issue you are fighting is a local tax increase, everyone in your grassroots organization should be armed with three egregious examples of waste and fraud in local government.

ASSUME THE MORAL HIGH GROUND

When you make comments, whether in informal conversations, addressing a political body, or speaking with the media, assume that anyone in their right mind agrees with you, and show that assumption in a confident demeanor. Speak with a tone and posture that says you are on the side of common sense, and that common sense needs no defense. The burden of argument and defense is on those who are at odds with the mainstream. Remember the Three Rs technique to turn any attack against the attackers.

You can use your three big issues tactically to put the left on the defensive and to define the terms of the debate for uninformed voters. Three issues are easy to remember, and something about three things in a row seems to create a mental rhythm that adds extra punch.

You can also use your big three issues in a more strategic fashion to force the left to fight on multiple fronts. Though you never want to become unfocused, you want to have a coordinated attack that maximizes your resources and scatters those of the left.

THREE ROLLING DEMANDS

We suggest that your agenda include three issues that roll through the spotlight. One issue will always be in sharp focus, but there will be two others on the periphery. You might actually have a number of strategic goals that you want to accomplish with your group, but it will help to bring them out three at a time.

Let's continue with education as an example. Suppose your group's first three concerns are

1. A biased textbook
2. A small number of left-wing teachers who are known to push their political views in class
3. A bloated administrative budget

Now imagine that the left has begun to push for tax increases to raise teacher pay. Imagine that one of our own on the school board is hit with the traditional "How can you say that you support education when you oppose tax increases to pay our teachers?"

Let's practice the Three Rs technique:

- *Recognize:* What is the debate the liberals want to have? They want you to prove that you support education even though you don't support tax increases. They want you to start on the defensive, as in, "Of course I support education, but I'm concerned that the taxpayers are struggling. . . ." If you go that route, you are on the defensive and you have already lost.
- *Reframe:* What is the debate *you* want to have, the one that puts the liberals on the defensive? We want them to have to prove that more money is the only way to improve education. So a good reframe would be, "When will we get past the tired old dogma that throwing more money at our problems will fix them?" Notice that you have used language that equates "tax increase" with "throwing more money." You have also planted the seed that there are problems that are being ignored.
- *Refocus:* Now focus attention on your agenda. "Parents are telling us that the political bias in our textbooks is unfair, that we have a small number of teachers who abuse their authority by pushing their political viewpoints in class, and that our lavish administrative overhead takes money away from our hardworking teachers. It seems grossly unfair to working families to talk about tax increases while we ignore the concerns of those who are footing the bill."

Notice how the liberals started out on the offensive, but now they will clearly be on the defensive. Even if they ridicule the parents who have raised the concerns, they are on the defensive. Keep them on the defensive by hammering these three themes in your public comments. That way, liberals sense that you are on to them, they see that parents are fired up, and they begin to struggle with the problem of how they can defend against all three attacks. Now you start with the camel's nose.

ISSUE 1 IN FOCUS (ISSUES 2 AND 3 IN BACKGROUND)

You have raised three issues in the Refocus step above, but you will focus 90 percent of your early effort on Issue 1, the biased textbook. Complaints to the school board, letters to the editor, calls to talk radio—whatever your method, keep the focus on Issue 1. You might mention Issues 2 and 3 ten percent of the time as part of introductory statements, to keep those issues alive, and to divert some of the left's resources to preparing a defense of those issues. Think of Issues 2 and 3 at this point as diversionary. The only issue on which you actually make a specific demand is Issue 1, and you work tirelessly to get some compromise in your favor.

Once the left agrees to the compromise goal, work on implementing that, and let things cool down for a while. Your group works for a living, so they cannot be full-time activists. Let the liberals think that their small concession quieted you down.

Then you do your Detective Columbo impression: "Oh, just one more thing . . ." That's when you find a way to improve upon the compromise goal. Maybe the school board agreed to make supplemental history texts available, so now you begin to question whether there are enough texts, and whether all students are really getting the benefits of having diverse materials available to them. Up the ante. Now you want the school to buy and provide the supplemental texts for *all* history students. Again, you might fall back to a compromise, maybe that each student will do one project during the year that is based on the supplemental texts.

See the pattern? Demand what you won't get, and compromise to get the nose under the tent. Then, when they've grown accustomed to what you got last time, come back and repeat the process. Each time, you gain a little ground and they lose a little ground. And occasionally,

Issues 2 and 3 come up in introductory comments or in sidebar comments. But they're always in the background.

Now, when you have made substantial progress on Issue 1, it's time to shift the focus.

ISSUE 2 IN FOCUS (ISSUES 1 AND 3 IN BACKGROUND)

Now change your focus so that 90 percent of your airtime is on Issue 2, the abuse by some teachers of their position by pushing their political biases on their students. There are only two groups: the mainstream teachers, parents, and administrators who want fairness in education, and the small number of leftist teachers who abuse their trust. Demand their dismissal, then compromise and agree to clarified standards and an anonymous complaint process for students and parents.

Meanwhile, you have built some momentum on Issue 1 and you occasionally come back and move that one a little further along: "Just one more thing; I'm sure it's nothing. . . ." Maybe you add a supplemental text or two about the original intent of the Constitution, or the real history of the slave trade—Islamic and Latino countries took far more slaves from Africa than did the United States, which casts a shadow over the liberal version of slavery as a uniquely American evil. But these compromises are now mostly out of the public view. The public attention is on ensuring that good and fair teachers don't have to work alongside a handful of bad apples.

Suppose you have demanded dismissal of these teachers and then settled for an anonymous complaint process. Now you up the ante and demand "fairness and balance" standards with which all teachers must comply, then compromise and settle for guidelines for fairness and balance.

For now.

ISSUE 3 IN FOCUS (ISSUES 2 AND 4 IN BACKGROUND)

By now you should also have made enough progress on Issue 2 that you can move this one to the background. Now put 90 percent of your public focus on the third issue, reducing administrative overhead and putting that money into rewarding teachers who have the fewest "fairness and balance" complaints or into funding special training. About this time, begin to introduce Issue 4. Maybe that could be a demand that all teachers attend special sensitivity training to "expand their appreciation of diverse approaches to American History."

You know the drill by now. Demand, compromise, repeat.

Always keep three issues on the table, with one getting 90 percent of the focus. As you see progress, move the spotlight onto a new issue.

Does that sound unworkable or cumbersome? This tactic has worked for the left for decades. Look back at the Obama regime: bailouts, cap and trade, health care. When the bailouts were a done deal, the focus was cap and trade, health care, and amnesty. Even when they lost cap and trade in Congress, they continued to advance it through regulation, and then the focus was raising the debt ceiling so that they could continue spending.

This stuff has worked for the left for years. Now the mainstream must make it work in the interest of restoring our constitutional republic. Never forget: Our camel is bigger than their camel, and we're paying for the tent.

10

IT'S FOR THE CHILDREN

The left controls our formal educational institutions, but they do not yet control our homes and hearths. Much education takes place outside formal institutions, in the values and habits that children learn at home, by the heroes we celebrate and the legends we share. The battle for America will be won or lost not just in our schools and other institutions of culture, but also in our living rooms, around our dinner tables, and in the bedtime stories that we tell our children.

PRINCIPLE 7: INOCULATE CHILDREN AGAINST LIBERALISM.

Mainstream parents who deliberately plan and guide the education and acculturation of their children will have a better chance of raising tomorrow's reinforcements in the struggle against liberal dominance. And given the tax burden of supporting government-run schools, most Americans will not be able to homeschool or to send their children to private schools. So we have to find ways to ensure that children learn our worldview and our real history even as they attend government schools run by liberals.

Children are easy to influence. That is why liberals targeted the halls of education as a critical piece of their Long March strategy.

TRUSTING MINDS, SIMPLE MESSAGE

Take a moment to consider why children are easy to influence. First, they don't know what they don't know. For example, if a teacher tells them that Roosevelt ended the Great Depression with his massive public spending programs, they simply absorb that information as fact. After all, why wouldn't they? Children don't know that there's overwhelming evidence that Roosevelt's programs prolonged the Great Depression by several years. To children raised with the Roosevelt myth, massive "stimulus" spending in response to an economic slowdown will sound reasonable to them later in life, as if it is tried-and-true medicine instead of economic insanity.

If children hear of the "Red Scare" as a period in which paranoid Americans worried needlessly about communist infiltration in our government, if Senator Joseph McCarthy is vilified, then liberals only need to scream "McCarthyism!" in order to silence anyone who points out the radicalism of their positions.

Second, young students tend to bond with their teachers. Remember our discussion of the biological and emotional basis for the development of a childhood conscience? Children learn to feel good when authority figures are happy with them and to feel guilty when authority figures are disappointed. Teachers are authority figures, and children are wired to want to please them and stay on their good side. For most of their formative years, children spend more time with teachers than with their parents.

Let us be clear that we in no way wish to paint all teachers as liberals. In fact, mainstream teachers will be the first to tell you that liberals dominate our system. They will tell you about required Muslim Sensitivity Training and the telling absence of Christian Sensitivity Training. Often, these mainstream teachers simply work beneath the radar. Most will admit to fear of intimidation or retaliation if the wrong colleagues were to find out about their mainstream views.

There are also teachers who never intended to be political activists. They just wanted to teach, and they unknowingly absorbed the assumptions and worldview of the leftists in the Department of Education. They just teach what is in the curriculum, and, of course, that curriculum is designed by hardcore leftists.

LIBERALISM IS EASIER THAN WISDOM

There is another reason that children are vulnerable to liberal ideas. Simply put, liberal ideas are childish ideas, and in some ways liberal rhetoric is more appealing than conservative reality. Which sounds better to a young child, that you have to work hard for what you get or that there is a kind person who will spread the wealth around?

Mainstream thinking is mature thinking, and it is more complex. Mainstream thinking captures the wisdom accumulated by generations of our predecessors. They teach us through fables and stories that our actions have short- and long-term consequences. As we mature, we learn that things that feel good in the short term may have dangerous long-term ramifications. We learn that many of the things that we want take time to get, and that we have to earn them; we are not entitled to them. We learn that tampering with something that we don't understand in order to improve it will invariably make it worse. We no longer think that we can change reality by wishing. We learn limits.

The fact that liberalism is an easy fit for the childlike mind and the fact that teachers have such powerful influence over children suggests the need for a careful strategy when working to reform education. We want to undermine the liberal indoctrination that our children receive in school without undermining their respect for *legitimate* authority.

GUERILLA EDUCATION

Though the specifics are of course up to each parent, we offer some general guidelines and methods that can help to get mainstream children through liberal schools without setting them up for retaliation or undermining their respect for adult authority. We call our approach "Guerilla Education."

The key to everything that follows is for parents to be mindful and deliberate in shaping the education and acculturation of children who will be exposed to heavy doses of liberal dogma. Some general principles follow.

FRONT-LOADING VALUES

Liberals have become alarmed that exposure to celebrations such as the Fourth of July can predispose children to conservative political values.[61] That is good news, indeed.

The greater the young child's emotional attachment to the stories, symbols, rituals, and values of mainstream America, the more difficult it will be to shake that attachment later. You can tell the stories of America's founding and our heroes in ways that are age-appropriate and that embed desirable values in the childhood conscience, and you can start doing so before the child starts school. Pay particular attention to heroes like George Washington, Thomas Jefferson, and others who will be minimized at best and discredited at worst by liberal institutions.

Make sure children have strongly positive associations with the Fourth of July. Slip in some simple teaching with the hot dogs and fireworks. Find age-appropriate ways to not only explain Memorial Day but also to honor it. In so doing, you are planting seeds deep in the child's limbic brain, in his or her deep conscience, that America is a good country and that our heroes are good people. Be sure that, in age-appropriate ways, the child learns that liberty and personal responsibility are linked.

Some of the old fables make great bedtime stories and provide powerful teaching opportunities. "The Ant and the Grasshopper" is a great chance to teach the implications of liberty and personal responsibility, that the decisions one makes have consequences, and it's done in an entertaining way. Both characters had the freedom to use their time as they wished, but the grasshopper wasted his time while the ant saved up food for the winter. This story perfectly illustrates why it's unfair to "spread the wealth" around if someone doesn't like the results of his decisions.

Make sure that you draw connections that are relevant to the child's experience. When the child has shown patience and determination and has finally reached a goal, remind her of the ants who worked and then had lots of food. Make sure she gets the parallel.

A child's interest in sports can also provide fertile ground for embedding conservative political values. Remember Churchill's statement that the Battle of Britain was won on the playing fields of Eton. In addition to the exercise benefits, involvement in sports provides an opportunity to teach children self-discipline, that perseverance pays off, and also that sometimes we have to dust ourselves off and move on.

It is also an opportunity to help the child to understand that everyone does not have the same talents in all areas, and that it is up to us to find those areas in which we can excel.

"IN ADDITION TO WHAT YOUR BOOK SAYS . . ."

As the child gets into school, and as you monitor what is being taught in their textbooks, you will begin to see the distortions and omissions that have been so well documented by mainstream researchers. There is no need to try to explain to grade-school children that their textbooks contain indoctrination. They are too young to understand, and you will only create unnecessary doubt and confusion. But you can *supplement* what is in their books, especially if you have done those things that we mentioned above. You will have already established "talking about our country and our values" as a normal and interesting thing you do in your house, so it should not seem odd to them when you look at their textbooks and engage them in discussion.

The Politically Incorrect Guide series of books is an excellent resource. With younger students, concentrate more on implanting correct information than on disputing incorrect information. Grade-school children are unlikely to be interested in noticing the contradictions between what they are learning at school and what they are learning at home, and there is no need to emphasize the contradictions yet. You can just put different ideas side by side. The spirit is, "Here's some more information I found about the Great Depression." You can always add, "This adds some information that wasn't in your book." You do not have to say *why* the additional information wasn't in their textbook.

When they get old enough and interested enough to notice that one source says FDR stopped the Great Depression and the other one says he made it worse, you can legitimately begin teaching that different scholars sometimes have different points of view, and the ones who wrote the textbook obviously had an opinion that not everyone shares. You are not yet discussing deliberate political bias, but you are planting a healthy recognition that just because something is in a textbook, it isn't necessarily the last word on a topic. You have also made your children aware that not every expert thinks FDR was great, for example, something they would never have heard if you hadn't made that information available at the right time.

At this stage, you can always use the lingo of the left to make your point: Looking at the opinions of different sources shows critical thinking skills and valuing diverse points of view. It is too early to teach your children that liberals define "critical thinking skills" as "criticizing America," and "valuing diverse points of view" as "not disagreeing with liberals." So in telling children that it is good to think critically and that an example of critical thinking is to look at several sources, you are actually using the normal definition of the phrase. You will have softened the impact of liberal indoctrination without undermining the teacher or the school.

EDUCATION ISN'T JUST FOR SCHOOL

There are many opportunities to teach children in a relatively structured way outside of the school system. Traditional churches could easily have Sunday school classes that incorporate teaching about the religious foundations of our country, the interpretation of the First Amendment's establishment clause for the first two centuries of American life, the real history of Thanksgiving, or other topics that are appropriate for Sunday school and would also give children a more accurate and complete picture of our country than what they learn in school.

Again, no one has to say, "Your teachers are filling your heads with liberal dogma." The idea is that different scholars emphasize different points and have different agendas. Any doubt is thereby focused on the text and the materials, and not on the teachers with whom your children might have bonded. There are excellent resources on intelligent design that could be very useful as part of a Sunday school series designed for children. If mainstream teachers attend the church, they would be obvious resources for such classes.

The Tea Party movement is another potential vehicle for guerilla education. When you find examples of bias in texts, be sure to alert others in the movement. When you find good resources for challenging the bias, share that information as well.

There is another advantage to using Sunday schools, Tea Party events, or other mainstream social gatherings as opportunities for teaching: Because there will be other young people there, your child is likely to develop peers whose parents are in the mainstream and who are learning mainstream values themselves. The positive peer group can help to reduce the influence of peers who swallow the leftist dogma.

MAKING THE CONSCIOUS CHOICE

By junior high, your children should have a solid visceral attachment to America's values and heroes. They should also have learned valuable information that is not presented in liberal textbooks. If you are politically active, you probably will have talked about your political beliefs at home and maybe even taken your children along to political functions. With the emotional foundation well established, it is time to elaborate upon the intellectual superstructure. That is the point at which you can begin to talk openly with your children about liberty versus tyranny.

The inevitable questions will come up about people your children know and like who are openly liberal—some of whom will be popular teachers or peers—and you can make good use of our concept of the politically uninformed and misinformed. It is important for children to realize that good people can be misinformed, especially when they have only heard one side of the story. The more mainstream peers your children have, through the Tea Party or other grassroots movements, the less they will be pulled by the liberal peer pressure within the schools.

11

WILL THE GIANT GO BACK TO SLEEP?

We are fully aware that what we have recommended is alien to the character of the mainstream majority. Mainstream Americans are not political animals. We meet our needs for control and power by developing control and power over our own selves and managing our own lives, not by dominating others.

As things stand now, it is hard enough to get mainstreamers out to the polls, but it is indeed a sobering thought that, as long as we share a country with radical leftists bent on imposing their will on us, whether we live as citizens or subjects will depend on getting the historically passive mainstream majority mobilized in support of liberty and constitutional government.

THE PRICE

If you choose to resist liberal rule, be fully aware that the left does not tolerate diversity. You will risk ostracism and ridicule at a minimum. If you are a student, your grades could be adversely affected. If you have a career or a business, you may find them targeted for attack by liberals in positions of power.

And that's if you're a behind-the-scenes activist. If your role is a public one, such as holding elected office or leading a community group, harassment from the IRS is a possibility. Bizarre as it appears to normal Americans, Homeland Security might even keep an eye on you.[62] That's far easier and safer for the liberals in charge than going after Islamic terrorists. Besides, Islamic terrorists and liberals have a common enemy: the Judeo-Christian foundations of mainstream American culture. And never forget that liberal tactics are not constrained by conscience, as we would understand the term. Threats of violence and even actual violence are often directed at anyone who gets in the way of liberals fulfilling their lust for power.

We are not reminding you of the dangers of resistance in order to discourage you, but to inform you. Liberals have shown their hand. There is no excuse for expecting them to do anything but what they have said they will do. If anyone gets in their way, liberals will do whatever they can to get what they want, "by any means necessary," as they promised repeatedly throughout the violent sixties.

WHAT IS BIGGER THAN YOUR FEAR?

There is another reason for reminding you of what you will face. If you are like us, you have a deep sense that what liberals have been doing in America is more than wrong-headed, it is just plain *wrong*. The contradictions between their self-righteous proclamations and their actions just reek of hypocrisy and amorality. That deep sense of the moral wrongness of liberalism and the rightness of liberty will at times be the only thing standing between you and surrender.

When you are face-to-face with liberal hatred, you can expect to feel fear. You will probably feel all the urges that we've discussed throughout this book: to explain yourself, to defend common sense, and even to appease liberals in order to get them out of your face. You will feel, in all likelihood, the urge to go back to the lawnmower and let others do the political work.

After all, mainstream Americans are peaceful people, and politics can be rough-and-tumble. But to restore the cultural foundations of liberty, you will have to have a clear sense that something is bigger than your fear. That's what will enable us to risk "our lives, our fortunes, and our sacred honor," as did our founders in the Declaration of Independence.

So, for you, what is bigger than the fear of being hated by angry leftists? We offer the following questions to help you to hone in on what outweighs your fear of what liberals might say and do:

- What motivated you to buy and read this book in the first place?
- Regardless of what the future holds, when you look back on these critical days in America's history, how do you want to remember your actions?
- If America in the future is totally dominated by the radical left, who in your life will be most harmed?

The last question is especially important. Our actions today will determine not only how our loved ones live in the near future but also what kind of government we pass on to the next generation.

OUR CONCORD BRIDGE MOMENT

We have used a number of battle metaphors to describe the struggle for America's future. We hope you will bear with us as we end with just one more.

On April 19, 1775, American colonists met and defeated British soldiers at Concord Bridge in Lexington, Massachusetts. Many of us read in school about the colonial heroism of that day and formed an image of a small band of patriots who met and defeated a larger British unit. But the truth is that the colonists vastly outnumbered the British troops at that battle.

That may seem to detract from the heroism of those patriots, but it actually does nothing of the sort. In fact, Concord Bridge provides a good metaphor for mainstream citizens who outnumber the far left but have been dominated by their policies, just as those colonists were dominated by a foreign minority.

And, though they outnumbered the British forces, those patriots were going up against the government of King George III, and the king was not going to surrender power without a fight. Yes, the prospect of short-term victory in that first battle was good because of the numerical superiority of the colonists, but the long-term picture was different indeed. The British met disloyalty to the Crown with unimaginable brutality. Many of their fellow colonists preferred the devil they knew—rule by a distant and arrogant government—to the uncertainty of founding a new system. Those patriots truly risked everything they had on that bridge.

When we see heroic images of the Battle of Concord Bridge in books and paintings, we can turn the page in the book or turn our heads from the painting, and the scene changes for us. We go back to our climate-controlled reality and a well-stocked refrigerator. But it might help us to remember, as we face our own choice today, that the scene did not change for the patriots at Concord Bridge. The smell of fear, the threat of death, and the desire to be doing anything but starting a protracted struggle with one of the mightiest armies on the face of the earth—those were all too real. Those patriots were needed and missed at home, and the pull of home, hearth, and family haunted them with every step they took.

Yes, victory was sweet at Concord Bridge. But along the road from the victory at Concord Bridge to the victory at Yorktown lay that winter at Valley Forge. Fear was bad enough, the pull of home and hearth were tempting enough, but Valley Forge added hunger and frostbite.

Rest assured that those of us in today's patriot movement will have our Concord Bridge moments, as we did in November of 2010, and we hope to have our political Yorktown, when it is clear that our constitutional republic is safe for at least one more generation. But rest assured that we will also face our Valley Forge moments, as a movement and possibly also as individuals.

So why did those early patriots stand their ground during that hard winter, when victory was anything but assured? The common answer is that they stayed to give us our liberty and our Constitution, but that answer ignores human nature. Our ideals are real enough when we are warm and safe, but they are distant thoughts at best in the face of freezing temperatures, hunger, and the horror of battle. Those intellectual ideals were responsible for the patriots' *enlistment* in the cause in the first place, in the warm days of spring, but not for *staying* in the fight when times were cold and hard.

We believe that patriots throughout our history have enlisted because of their ideals, but those patriots stayed in the fight because of loyalty to the people beside them and love for the people at home. Love of family and friends, and a deep desire not to let their family and friends down, were reasons that our troops have fought our nation's enemies for over two hundred years. A sense of conscience, that it would be *wrong* to leave the cause and to let family and friends down, was the reason that our troops stayed during those times when their intellectual ideals were obscured by the fog of battle.

Humans are social creatures, and much of what we do is a result of our social bonds. Yes, we are trying to restore a constitutional republic, and intellectually we believe that is the right thing to do. But when we face liberal hatred, when we start to hear discord within our ranks, when progress seems slow, the only thing that will keep us going will be our commitment to those we love, because they will live with the consequences of our actions.

Join the struggle, if you haven't already, because of your commitment to the principles upon which this country was founded. But stay in the struggle through those moments of doubt and discouragement, because that is the best thing you can do for those you love.

Our battle will be fought not with the technology of war, not even with the technology of civics, but with the technology of politics. The outcome of our struggle will be just as important for us and for future generations as was the outcome at Concord Bridge and that winter at Valley Forge, because we will decide whether Americans will live as subjects of a government or citizens of a republic.

May God give us the strength and courage to do what is necessary to restore legitimate constitutional government in America. If we fail, we will be the last generation of Americans to know those blessings.

But, if we succeed, we will join previous generations of patriots who secured the blessings of liberty for themselves and for us. Now it is up to us to secure the blessings of liberty for ourselves and for posterity.

ENDNOTES

1   Richard M. Weaver, *Ideas Have Consequences* (Chicago, IL: University of Chicago Press, 1948).

2   This poem has long been a favorite of conservative thinkers because of its emphasis on timeless wisdom. John Silber included the whole poem in this 1989 book, *Straight Shooting: What's Wrong with America and How to Fix It*. Glenn Beck's video introducing *The Overton Window* included quotes from the poem as well.

3   See Derek Thompson, "Signs of Dissent: What About the 47% Who Pay No Federal Income Taxes?" (*theatlantic.com,* October 14, 2011).

4   See, for example, Michelle Malkin, "The Real Snow Job in DC: Obamacare Waivers Skyrocket to 729 + 4 States; 4 New SEIU Waiver Winners" (*michellemalkin.com*, January 26, 2011).

5   John Silber, *Straight Shooting: What's Wrong with America and How to Fix It* (New York, NY: Harper & Rowe, 1989). The opening chapter of Silber's excellent book provides an in-depth look at the wisdom that was transmitted from generation to generation through the copybooks and other educational methods.

6   Jonathan Allen and John Bresnahan, "Sources: Joe Biden Likened Tea Partiers to Terrorists" (*politico.com*, August 1, 2011).

7   See "Gov. Scott Walker Responds to Outrage Over Passing Wisconsin Union Bill" (*foxnews.com*, March 11, 2011).

8   Michael Savage, *Liberalism Is a Mental Disorder: Savage Solutions* (Nashville, TN: Nelson Current, 2005).

9   Lyle H. Rossiter, Jr., *The Liberal Mind: The Psychological Causes of Political Madness* (St. Charles, IL: Free World Books, LLC, 2006).

10 Ann Coulter, *Demonic: How the Liberal Mob Is Endangering America* (New York, NY: Crown Forum, 2011).

11 "Obama fires up Democrats: 'I want you to argue with them and get in their face'" (*nydailynews.com*, September 18, 2008).

12 Transcript from *The O'Reilly Factor* (*foxnews.com*, August 10, 2009).

13 See William S. Lind, "Who stole our culture?" (*Whistleblower Magazine*, June 2010); and Patrick J. Buchanan, *The Death of the West: How Dying Populations and Immigrant Invasions Imperil Our Country and Civilization* (New York, NY: Thomas Dunne Books, 2002).

14 Ravi Zacharias, *Deliver Us from Evil: Restoring the Soul in a Disintegrating Culture* (Nashville, TN: Word Publishing, 1997).

15 Hillary R. Clinton, "Children's Rights Under the Law" (*Harvard Educational Review*, November 1973).

16 David Limbaugh, *Persecution: How Liberals Are Waging War Against Christianity* (Washington, DC: Regnery Publishing, Inc., 2003).

17 Linda Kimball, "Cultural Marxism" (*americanthinker.com*, February 17, 2007).

18 See for example "Marriage: America's #1 Weapon Against Childhood Poverty" (*heritage.org*, Fall, 2010).

19 See the following for examples: Bernard Goldberg, *Bias: A CBS Insider Reveals How the Media Distort the News* (Washington, DC:

Regnery, 2002); Dinesh D'Souza, *Illiberal Education: The Politics of Race and Sex on Campus* (New York, NY: The Free Press, 1991); Thomas Sowell, *Inside American Education: The Decline, The Deception, The Dogmas* (New York, NY: The Free Press, 1993); and Tim Groseclose, *Left Turn: How Liberal Media Bias Distorts the American Mind* (New York, NY: St. Martin's Press, 2011).

20 "Review Ordered of Video Showing Students Singing Praises of President Obama" (*foxnews.com*, September 24, 2009).

21 *heraldsun.com*, May 26, 2011.

22 Bernard Goldberg, *Bias: A CBS Insider Reveals How the Media Distort the News* (Washington, DC: Regnery, 2002).

23 See for example Tim Graham, "Too Complex for Dummies? Ted Turner Explains Why 'Some People Don't Get It' on Global Warming" (*newsbusters.org*, June 26, 2011).

24 See for example Brad Wilmouth, "PBS's Gordon Peterson Suggests Dream Act Would Pass if Illegal Immigrants 'Looked Like Norwegians'" (*newsbusters.org*, December 25, 2010).

25 See for example Jeff Poor, "Behar Panel Celebrates First Year of Tea Party with Racist and Violent Labels" (*newsbusters.org*, March 02, 2010).

26 Larry Schweikart, *48 Liberal Lies about American History (That You Probably Learned in School)* (New York, NY: Sentinel, 2008).

27 See for example "Paper Calls Clarence Thomas 'Black Man with an Asterisk'" (*newsmax.com*, November 1, 2005).

28 See for example Star Parker, *Uncle Sam's Plantation: How Big Government Enslaves America's Poor and What We Can Do About It* (Nashville, TN: Thomas Nelson, 2003, 2010).

29 See Robert Rector, "Marriage: America's Greatest Weapon Against Child Poverty" (*heritage.org*, September 16, 2010).

30 Victor Davis Hanson, "The 'Racism' Canar" (*National Review* online, September 16, 2009).

31 Marcella Bombardieri, "Summers' Remarks on Women Draw Fire" (*boston.com*, January 17, 2005).

32 Patrick J. Buchanan, *The Death of the West: How Dying Populations and Immigrant Invasions Imperil Our Country and Civilization* (New York, NY: Thomas Dunne Books, 2002).

33 L. Brent Bozell, "Art in America: Bravo's Reality Show "Work of Art" Demonstrates our Popular Culture is Thoroughly Rotten" (*mrc.org*, July 10, 2010).

34 Patrick J. Buchanan, *The Death of the West: How Dying Populations and Immigrant Invasions Imperil Our Country and Civilization* (New York, NY: Thomas Dunne Books, 2002). See Chapter Eight for an excellent review of the left's targeting of Christian thinking and symbols.

35 See as an example the comment about the purpose of public museums in Brent Baker, "Hypocrisy on Parade: *NYT* Runs Photo of Dung-Clotted 'Virgin Mary'" (*mrc.org: Cyberalert*, Vol. 11; No. 25, February 9, 2006).

36 Saul D. Alinsky, *Rules for Radicals: A Political Primer for Realistic Radicals* (New York, NY: Random House, 1971).

37 Brian Sussman, *Climategate: A Veteran Meteorologist Exposes the Global Warming Scam* (Washington, DC: WND Books, 2010).

38 S. Fred Singer and Dennis T. Avery, *Unstoppable Global Warming: Every 1,500 Years* (Lanham, MD: Rowman and Littlefield Publishers, Inc., 2007).

39 Ezekiel 16:44, King James Version.

40 For an excellent overview of worldviews, see James W. Sire, *The Universe Next Door: A Basic Worldview Catalog, Fourth Edition* (Downers Grove, IL: InterVarsity Press, 2004).

41 See for example Brendan Sweetman, *Why Politics Needs Religion: The Place of Religious Arguments in the Public Square* (Downers Grove, IL: InterVaristy Press, 2006).

42 For a very readable overview, see Glenn S. Sunshine, *Why You Think the Way You Do: The Story of Western Worldviews from Rome to Home* (Grand Rapids, MI: Zondervan, 2009).

43 For a good overview of these and other early thinkers, see Colin Brown, *Philosophy & the Christian Faith: A Historical Sketch from the Middle Ages to the Present Day* (Downers Grove, IL: InterVarsity Press, 1968).

44 For an overview of the development of these views and their impact on psychological theory, see Richard Lowry, *The Evolution of Psychological Theory: 1650 to the Present* (Chicago, IL: Aldine Publishing Company, 1971).

45 See Chapter Three in James W. Sire, *The Universe Next Door: A Basic Worldview Catalog, Fourth Edition* (Downers Grove, IL: InterVarsity Press, 2004).

46 See Colin Brown, *Philosophy & the Christian Faith: A Historical Sketch from the Middle Ages to the Present Day* (Downers Grove, IL: InterVarsity Press, 1968).

47 Colin Brown, *Philosophy & the Christian Faith: A Historical Sketch from the Middle Ages to the Present Day* (Downers Grove, IL: InterVarsity Press, 1968).

48 Erik von Kuehnelt-Leddihn, *Leftism Revisited: From de Sade and Marx to Hitler and Pol Pot* (Washington, DC: Regnery Gateway, 1990).

49 See for example Robert J. Spitzer, *New Proofs for the Existence of God: Contributions of Contemporary Physics and Philosophy* (Grand Rapids, MI: Wm. B. Eerdmans Publishing Company, 2010) and Michael J. Behe, *Darwin's Black Box: The Biochemical Challenge to Evolution* (New York, NY: Simon and Schuster, 1996).

50 Ibid.

51 Whitaker Chambers, *Witness* (Washington, DC: Regnery Gateway, 1952).

52 Lyle H. Rossiter, Jr., *The Liberal Mind: The Psychological Causes of Political Madness* (St. Charles, IL: Free World Books, LLC, 2006).

53 It is fitting that the still, small voice that speaks to Elijah in 1 Kings 19:12 does so in the midst of tumult. In emotionally charged moments, that voice is quiet indeed, but it is there.

54 Russell Kirk, *The Conservative Mind: From Burke to Santayana* (Washington, DC: Regnery Publishing, Inc., 1985).

55 A good start for laypersons interested in this important theory is Wikipedia's article on Learned Helplessness: http://en.wikipedia.org/wiki/Learned_helplessness.

56 Russell Kirk, *The Conservative Mind: From Burke to Santayana* (Washington, DC: Regnery Publishing, Inc., 1985).

57 See Daniel Goleman, *Emotional Intelligence* (New York, NY: Bantam Books, 1995).

58 See the Fox News clip on YouTube, "Chris Christie vs. Teachers Unions": http://www.youtube.com/watch?v=yuri7p_9pm4.

59 See Walter Williams, "Victimhood: Rhetoric or Reality?" (*Jewish World Review*, June 8, 2005).

60 Thomas E. Woods, *The Politically Incorrect Guide to American History* (Washington, DC: Regnery, 2004).

61 See Rush Limbaugh, "Harvard Libs Admit Fourth of July Celebrations Are for Conservatives" (*rushlimbaugh.com*, June 30, 2011).

62 Teddy Davis and Ferdous Al-Faruque, "Napolitano Facing Republican Calls for Her Ouster" (*abcnews.go.com*, April 23, 2009).

22061216